DATE DUE

FEB 2 3 2006			
APR 0 3 2006			
SEP 1 2 2007			

CLIMATE OF FEAR

Why We Shouldn't Worry about Global Warming

Thomas Gale Moore

CATO INSTITUTE
Washington, D.C.

Library of Congress Cataloging-in-Publication Data

Moore, Thomas Gale.
   Climate of fear : Why we shouldn't worry about global warming /
Thomas Gale Moore.
     p.   cm.
   Includes bibliographical references and index.
   ISBN 1-882577-64-7 — ISBN 1-882577-65-5
   1. Global Warming.   2. Global Warming—Economic aspects.
I. Title.
QC981.8.G56M64   1998
363.738'74—dc21

                                       96-3143
                                         CIP

CATO INSTITUTE
1000 Massachusetts Ave., N.W.
Washington, D.C. 20001

Contents

ACKNOWLEDGMENTS   vii

INTRODUCTION   1

1. THE SCIENCE BEHIND PREDICTIONS OF CLIMATE CHANGE   9

2. HISTORICAL EVIDENCE ON CLIMATE AND HUMAN WELL-BEING   23

3. THE HEALTH EFFECTS OF GLOBAL WARMING   69

4. WEATHER BENEFITS AND OTHER ENVIRONMENTAL AMENITIES   89

5. THE ECONOMIC COSTS (BENEFITS?) OF A WARMER WORLD   103

6. SLOWING GREENHOUSE GAS EMISSIONS: POLITICS AND COSTS   129

REFERENCES   159

INDEX   169

Acknowledgments

I would like to thank my wife, Cassandra Chrones Moore, who read every word several times. She improved the grammar, caught mistakes, pointed out sections that were unclear, and made the work flow more smoothly. Without her careful and expert help, this book would be much less readable. Any remaining inadequacies are my responsibility.

A condensed version of Chapter 2 was published as "Why Global Warming Would Be Good for You" in *The Public Interest*, Winter 1995. Certain sections of Chapters 3 through 6 appeared first in various issues of *World Climate Report*.

Introduction

The whole aim of practical politics is to keep the populace alarmed (and hence clamorous to be led to safety) by menacing it with a series of hobgoblins.

H. L. Mencken

Does a Saturday afternoon barbecue, driving to church on Sunday, or enjoying a heaping plate of risotto contribute to the destruction of civilization, the ecology, and human life? Many of our most distinguished leaders, illustrious periodicals, and eminent scientists profess so. Vice President Al Gore has divined that the threat of global warming, resulting from human production of greenhouse gases, is "the most serious problem our civilization faces" (Healy 1994). (I wonder where he ranks nuclear proliferation, rising ethnic tensions, and the escalating gap between the world's rich and poor.) President Bill Clinton has warned:

> We simply must halt global warming. It is a threat to our health, to our ecology and to our economy. The problem frankly affects every sector of the economy (Clinton 1993).

A media chorus, led by such prestigious organizations as the *New York Times*, the Public Broadcasting System, and *Scientific American*, has fanned the fear of climate change. Reputable scientists, including Bert Bolin (Stockholm University), Benjamin Santer (Lawrence Livermore National Laboratory), Robert Watson (Office of Science and Technology Policy, White House), and Stephen Schneider (Stanford University) have claimed that the climate is changing or will shift and that measures are urgently needed to head off potential disaster. If these prophets are accurate, we must move quickly to slash the emission of greenhouse gases. Before we leap, however, we should be clear that such policies, which may be unnecessary, would be inordinately expensive and would lead to worldwide recession, rising unemployment, civil disturbances, and increased tension

1

between nations as accusations of cheating and violations of international treaties inflamed passions.

If the United States heeds those advocates, the risks will be exorbitant. Potential policies to reduce emissions threaten the energy that propels our economy, our cars, and our factories while heating and cooling our homes and making life easier, safer, and more humane. Those prophets would have us burn less fuel, give up our autos, turn down our thermostats in winter, turn them up in summer, travel less, and spend vast amounts of money on new and unproved technologies to cut the use of fossil fuels.

Strangely enough, if you believe the prognosticators right now, we live in the "best of all possible worlds," at least as far as climate goes. In the 1970s, many scientists worried about global cooling (Rasool and Schneider). The Department of Transportation organized a multiyear research effort involving hundreds of scientists and economists to evaluate its effects. The researchers found that a cooling of the world would reduce living standards. Since many of those same forecasters now predict doom from warming, we are obviously living on the edge between a world that is too hot and one that is too cold. Given that mankind, over the last million or so years, has evolved in climates that were both hotter and colder than today's, how is it that we in the 20th century are so fortunate as to have been born into the ideal global climate?

Many environmentalists have recommended that the United States and other nations adopt "no-regrets" policies that supposedly make sense in and of themselves, such as encouraging energy conservation, more fuel-efficient vehicles, and greater use of public transit (NRC 1991). They claim that energy-saving steps and greater efficiency would more than pay for themselves. Experience with similar initiatives, however, proves that they would be far from the free lunch suggested.

If a no-regrets policy were adopted and failed to make much of an impact on emission of greenhouse gases, as seems likely, environmental activists would push for stronger steps. How could they do otherwise if the effects of global climate change are as grim as they suggest? Consequently, a no-regrets program will be the first expensive and ineffectual step down the road to programs that will cripple one of the most vital foundations of modern civilization—our energy supplies.

Even if significant warming were to occur, public policymakers could, at the time it became evident, launch programs to adapt to the change, such as building dikes, increasing air conditioning, and aiding farmers and ecosystems to adjust to the new weather. To justify adopting policies now to abate the emission of greenhouse gases, proponents must show that, after programs to mitigate any damage are adopted, the resulting costs in lower living standards for Americans will be less than the costs of warming. What is often overlooked is the strong possibility that global warming would turn out to be beneficial. If climate change actually makes people better off, spending now to slow emissions would be wrong-headed.

Whether mankind should take steps to reduce the emission of greenhouse gases, such as carbon dioxide, methane, and nitrous oxides—under the Montreal Protocol, chlorofluorocarbons are already being phased out—depends on an uncertain future. What is the probability that such emissions will affect the global climate? How might the climate change and by how much? Given a menu of expected changes in typical weather, what are the probable effects on humans?

Climatologists do not agree on the effect of greenhouse gases on climate. For an effective doubling of CO_2, the United Nations' Intergovernmental Panel on Climate Change (IPCC) and many other experts predict a likely increase in average temperatures from 2.5° to 6.5° Fahrenheit, with the most likely boost being 4.5°. Other climatologists, such as Richard Lindzen (MIT), S. Fred Singer (Science and Environmental Policy Project), and Patrick Michaels (University of Virginia), predict negligible or only small warming. Nevertheless, most researchers do believe that, if man continues to seed the atmosphere with CO_2, climate change will occur, if it has not already started. Change is normally feared, thus many are apprehensive at the prospect. It is also true that people believe what it is in their interest to believe. If global climate change is viewed as a threat, environmental organizations can raise more support from the public; politicians can posture as protectors of mankind; newspapers can write more scary stories, thus increasing circulation; and scientists, even those most skeptical, can justify research grants to study the issue.

Economic forecasts of the influence of climate change on human activity also vary considerably. Some predict that people will benefit from any such change while others view the possibility with great alarm. As noted, Vice President Gore imagines the direst of consequences. Many of those who calculate small effects in the long run assert that the rate of climate change is unprecedented, at least in recorded history, and may create havoc over the next century. Apocalyptic forecasts catch people's attention; predictions of good weather elicit no more than a yawn.

As an economist, I will not attempt to judge the argument over the effect of greenhouse gases on the climate. The contention that more of those gases will lead to warming seems plausible, but the magnitude of the change appears uncertain. Every few years the major forecasts of warming over the next century have been revised downward. This book assumes that warming may occur over the next hundred years and will focus, consequently, on evaluating the effects of possible changes in climate and the costs of various strategies to slow any shifts in weather patterns. Although some Cassandras have projected rising greenhouse gas emissions for the next two or three hundred years to depict the dire consequences of scorching temperatures, this book will ignore such very, very long run potential apocalypses. We have no idea what the world will be like in a hundred years, much less two or three hundred. There is no sensible way to plan for such periods.

Furthermore, history and research support the proposition that a warmer climate is beneficial. Past warm periods have seen dramatic improvements in civilization and human well-being. Fortunately, President Clinton is wrong: our modern industrial economy is less affected by weather than are societies heavily dependent on nature. Higher average temperatures can bring many benefits, including longer growing seasons, a healthier and longer-lived population, and reduced transportation and communication costs. Although not everyone will find a warmer climate in his or her interest, the evidence shows that most individuals, especially those living in higher latitudes, will experience a gain. Climate change will probably be small in tropical areas, so the population of equatorial regions will be largely unaffected.

International Actions

Notwithstanding the evidence that a warmer climate might be beneficial and the absence of strong indications that the climate is changing, international pressures to stem greenhouse gas emissions are growing. At the Rio conference in 1992, most nations of the world signed the United Nations Framework Convention on Climate Change (FCCC), pledging themselves to voluntary steps to curb carbon emissions at 1990 levels by the year 2000. Although the Bush administration refused to commit to the goals and timetables of the convention, it signed the agreement and proposed a "no-regrets" policy. The Senate ratified the Convention in October of 1992.

Upon taking office in 1993, the Clinton administration quickly agreed to the aims of the Convention and, in the fall of 1993, issued a *Climate Change Action Plan* to meet the goals set forth at the Rio "Earth Summit," which were to stabilize "greenhouse gas concentrations in the atmosphere at a level that would prevent dangerous anthropogenic interference with the climate system." The Clinton plan relied on an extensive list of voluntary actions by industry, public utilities, and major energy consumers. The administration also proposed new building codes to save on energy as well as the planting of trees to absorb CO_2 emissions. The EPA Administrator, Carol M. Browner, promised the imposition of mandatory measures if the voluntary steps failed.

The Convention divides the world into three categories: the advanced industrialized countries, who are members of the OECD; those countries which were formerly part of the Soviet Empire and are currently transitioning to a market economy; and the rest of the world, that is, the Third World. The agreement required that the OECD countries take the most stringent steps, reducing their emissions of CO_2 to 1990 levels, while those who are "transitioning to a market economy" were given more latitude. The Third World, which includes such giants and fast growing states as China, Indonesia, India, Brazil, and Mexico, need not make any commitments. The industralized West must also furnish technology and funds to developing countries to encourage them to reduce emissions.

The 1992 Climate Change Convention created the Conference of Parties (COP), consisting of all states that ratified the agreement, to monitor compliance and adopt amendments and protocols to further the objectives of the treaty. The Convention provided for an international secretariat, a new UN bureaucracy, to administer the COP. (Governments love new organizations, more faceless bureaucrats, and new opportunities to find work for their supporters.)

At COP's first meeting in the spring of 1995, the "Berlin Mandate," which specifically excludes developing countries from any controls, laid out a path for negotiations toward a protocol on future greenhouse gas emissions restrictions. The agreement, signed in December of 1997, aims to cut emissions below 1990 levels, at least for the advanced industrialized countries.

Timothy Wirth, the undersecretary of state for global affairs, admitted in Berlin that the United States in the year 2000 might be 30 percent over the 1990 level. Notwithstanding his admission, Wirth in July 1996 asserted in Geneva the need for "binding targets." During 1997, the diplomatic circuit was extraordinarily busy attempting to negotiate a protocol to be signed in Kyoto at the end of the year. Whether anything should have been signed and whether the agreement should be ratified by the U.S. Senate is the subject of this book.

Costs versus Costs

This book evaluates public policy options, especially those being supported by the IPCC and environmental organizations. In considering what steps, if any, should be taken, the costs of acting must be weighed against the costs of continuing as normal. If the calculus shows that governments should adopt policies to cut the emission of greenhouse gases, the stringency of such programs must be determined. Cost/benefit analysis constitutes the only rational approach.

Although many environmentalists oppose cost/benefit analysis, it is the one sensible method of approaching public policy issues. If the cost of acting exceeds the gain from doing so, no steps are warranted. On the other hand, if the benefits from initiating a program to reduce the possibility of warming are greater than the expenses, the policy should be adopted. Logically, no reasonable being can oppose cost/benefit analysis; but environmentalists assert that the benefits, typically stated in monetary terms, overlook many ecological effects. How can one measure the value of a trout stream, winter snow in the Rocky Mountains, or a particular species of snail in New England? Can government bureaucrats put a price on human health, ecological vibrancy and species diversity, or the survival of tropical reefs? Although valuing these nonmarket concerns is extraordinarily difficult, consideration of the issues is vital. Environmentalists couch their appeals in emotional or religious terms; the "dismal science" should redress the balance.

Moreover, if steps are taken to reduce the emission of greenhouse gases, whether justified or not, they should be taken worldwide. A pound of CO_2 produced by backyard barbecues in Iowa has the same effect as a pound of CO_2 emitted from cooking stoves in India. The greenhouse gas problem is an example par excellence of a global commons issue. If China exploits its mammoth coal reserves to provide needed electricity for its billion people over the next century, the actions of the United States can have only a small effect on any future warming.

Even if society believes that warming will, on net, be harmful, restraining the emission of greenhouse gases by any one country or small group of countries makes sense only if most other nations follow suit. Should the United States impose taxes to reduce the use of fossil fuels, the benefit of doing so would be greater, the larger the number of other major nations joining in the restrictions. Free rider problems—that is, the temptation to leave the burden to others—may make international agreement to abate emissions difficult if not impossible.

Unfortunately, the expectation that climate change would have a differential effect on various nations exacerbates the free rider problem. The Russians, for example, have indicated that they would probably do well in a warmer world. On the other hand, island nations and countries with extensive low-lying land, such as Bangladesh, fear that global warming would be devastating. Certain poor nations, such as China, for example, consider economic development more important than warding off possible climate change.

At the Rio meeting in 1992, most industrialized countries agreed that steps to mitigate warming by slowing the emission of greenhouse gases were warranted. Serious disputes remain, however, over the measures necessary to cut emissions and the extent to which they should be cut. The most efficient method of meeting the Kyoto limits on emissions would require taxes on emissions of carbon; but problems would arise immediately. Since each country would have to impose its own levy, presumably in its own currency, the issue of comparability would be compounded by the need to determine appropriate exchange rates and to adjust for future market fluctuations in such rates. Moreover, nations with high existing tariffs on energy would demand that such levies be taken into account in setting the new charges.

Marketable quotas of carbon emissions could also be an efficient and low-cost method of reducing greenhouse gases and would, in principle, make meeting a particular emissions standard achievable. Jockeying over the initial allocation of those quotas, however, might undermine any accord. No single basis would command universal assent. Some nations would advocate reductions on a per-person basis; others, on existing emissions; and still others would claim credit for existing policies that restrict fossil fuel use.

As the reader will note, the subject of global climate change is far from simple. Not only must policymakers decide whether steps should be taken now to cut CO_2 emissions; but, should the political powers deem that necessary, they must reach an accord on the mechanisms and policies required. Agreement will be neither straightforward nor easy to implement.

Such policies would be extraordinarily expensive and would be likely to cause large-scale dislocations, unemployment, and economic stagnation. Fortunately, adopting such a program is unnecessary. For most people in the United States, Western Europe, Russia, and Japan, any climate change would probably be beneficial. A few poor countries that might suffer from rising sea levels or be unable to adjust their agriculture might suffer. If emissions controls are intended to protect those countries, it might be better to forgo the controls and target aid to promoting their economic development. However calculated, the cost of slowing warming exceeds by a substantial margin the benefits projected by even the most environmentally minded economists. Consequently the best strategy is to maintain the status quo, continue research on climate, and help poor countries improve their economies.

1. The Science behind Predictions of Climate Change

More than 100 years ago, a Swedish professor, Svante Arrhenius (1896), published the first paper pointing out that increases in carbon dioxide in the atmosphere might have effects on temperatures at ground level. He calculated—by hand—that if atmospheric concentrations of "carbonic acid," that is, carbon dioxide, were to increase by 50 percent, temperatures in the areas between 30 and 40 degrees north latitude would rise by 4.1°C (7.4° Fahrenheit) and on the oceans by 3.3°C (5.9°F), figures that differ very little from those currently projected on the basis of elaborate computer models. He believed that this would prove beneficial to far-northern countries, such as his own (Cogan 1992, 82).

Does science support the proposition that manmade greenhouse gases are leading to a climate change? In fact, the evidence for the claim that the earth has grown warmer is shaky: the theory is weak and the models on which the conclusions are based cannot even replicate the current climate.

Notwithstanding the IPCC's famous statement that "the balance of evidence suggests that there is a discernible human influence on global climate," the evidence fails to support the warming hypothesis (IPCC 1995d). Federal government statistics show no rise in temperatures (NOAA 1996). British naval records find no significant change in temperatures at sea since the mid-1800s (*Technological Review* 1989). The reported worldwide increases in temperature of 0.5° to 1.0°F since the late 19th century occurred mainly before 1940— before the rapid rise in CO_2. Moreover, for reasons explained later, those numbers are far from reliable for much of the period.

Even if we accept the figures showing that the world has become 1°F warmer, the computer models predict a much greater climb in temperature over the past 100 years than currently measured (Lindzen 1994). Even the National Academy of Sciences is skeptical of the validity of the computer models and warns that the modeling of clouds—a key climate factor—is inadequate and poorly understood (NRC 1991, 18). *Science* magazine has documented that the models need to be adjusted to replicate the current and past climates (Kerr 1994). Recently some researchers claim that by including aerosols the models fit the temperature records (Kerr 1995b). Patrick Michaels, a University of Virginia climatologist and a critic of global warming hysteria, has shown that the reported better fit resulted from using only a truncated portion of the record (Michaels 1997, 5–6). Even with aerosols in the model, the computer results fail to track temperatures over the last few years.

Generally Agreed On Facts

All climatologists agree that we live in a "greenhouse" world; the earth, were it not for the capture and retention of heat by components of the atmosphere, would be too cold to house most life forms, including humans. If the atmosphere did not trap heat, the earth's temperature would be about 70°F colder, much too low to support life (Lamb 1972, 49, n. 1). Water vapor is the main heat-retaining agent; it contributes about 98 percent of the greenhouse effect. In addition, carbon dioxide (CO_2), methane (CH_4), and, in the modern world, chlorofluorocarbons (CFCs) add to the effect. Most of the concern, however, has focused on the increases in atmospheric levels of carbon dioxide, a product of combustion. As mankind has increasingly relied on fossil fuels for energy, CO_2 emissions have climbed. An increase in methane, arising mainly from rice paddies and from domesticated animals, has also contributed to potential warming.

As Table 1-1 shows, most carbon dioxide comes from natural processes and all of it is recycled out of the atmosphere (Justus and Morrissey 1995). The oceans absorb much of it, although all sinks of CO_2 are not well identified. Human activity contributes only about 4.5 percent of total carbon emissions. Methane emissions from rice paddies, trash dumps, and domesticated animals produce yearly the equivalent in warming of between 3.3 and 5 billion metric tons of CO_2. Thus carbon dioxide and methane are currently contributing about 86 percent of all the greenhouse gases being added to the atmosphere (NRC 1991). CFCs and N_2O (nitrous oxide) constitute the remaining manmade warming gases. All these gases, produced by humans, warm the atmosphere slightly, leading to more evaporation and hence more water vapor (H_2O being the major molecule

Table 1-1
GLOBAL SOURCES AND ABSORPTION OF GREENHOUSE GASES
(millions of metric tons annually)

| Greenhouse Gas | Sources | | Absorption | Annual Increase of Gas in Atmosphere |
	Natural	Manmade		
CO_2	555,000	26,300	570,000	11,470–12,950
Methane	110–210	300–450	460–660	35–40
Nitrous Oxide	6–12	4–8	13–20	3–5

SOURCE: U.S. Energy Information Administration, *Emissions of Greenhouse Gases in the United States, 1995* (Washington: EIA, 1996). Cited in *Global Change* (electronic edition), March 1997; Pacific Institute for Studies in Development, Environment, and Security (http://www.globalchange.org).

that produces a warmer world). Scientists have estimated that concentrations of CO_2 and CH_4 are increasing about 0.5 percent (1.8 ppmv) and 0.9 percent (0.015 ppmv) annually (NRC 1991). About 40 percent of an increase in the emissions of carbon dioxide remains in the atmosphere for decades. The oceans promptly absorb but 15 percent; scientists are uncertain where the rest goes. It may be taken up as basic fertilizer by forests which, both in Europe and in the United States, have flourished in recent decades (Kauppi et al. 1992; Myneni et al. 1997). Climatologists estimate it would take between 50 and 200 years for a sudden injection of CO_2 into the atmosphere to be reabsorbed by the oceans and plants.

Methane and CFCs absorb more energy per molecule than does carbon dioxide and thus contribute more per molecule toward warming (see Table 1-2). Those emissions, however, constitute a smaller share of the total and thus add less to climate change. In fact, CFCs have been phased out in the industrial countries and are soon scheduled for complete abolition. CFCs also erode the ozone layer, a stratospheric phenomenon that contributes to a warmer climate. While CFCs absorb more energy, recent studies suggest that the added effect of this on climate change is roughly offset by their erosion of ozone (Justus and Morrissey 1995). On net, therefore, CFCs can be ignored: they are being phased out and they do not contribute much overall to climate change.

Table 1-2
DIRECT GLOBAL WARMING POTENTIAL FOR 100-YEAR
TIME HORIZON

Greenhouse Gas	Direct Global Warming	Indirect Component of Global Warming
Carbon Dioxide	1	none
Methane	11	positive
Nitrous Oxide	270	uncertain
CFC-11	3400	negative
CFC-12	7100	negative

SOURCE: IPCC 1992, 15, table 3.

Even though other gases retain more heat, most of the climatic effect of greenhouse gases comes from carbon dioxide. Of the direct heating of long-lived greenhouse gases, 64 percent comes from CO_2, while less than 20 percent comes from methane. According to the forecasts by the IPCC Working Group I, if carbon dioxide emissions remain at 1994 levels, atmospheric concentrations of that gas will reach about 500 parts per million of volume (ppmv) by the end of the next century, nearly twice the preindustrial level of 280 ppmv (IPCC 1995d).

In 1990, the National Academy of Sciences (NRC 1981) estimated that, if CO_2 emissions remained at current levels, the added warming would be about 1 watt per square meter (W/m^2) of the earth. In comparison, the sun's radiation striking the upper atmosphere has an average over the year of about 340 W/m^2. During a year, the earth radiates all of this back into space. Initially about 25 percent is reflected from the top of the atmosphere; 45 percent is absorbed at the earth's surface; about 5 percent is reflected from the oceans and from the earth's surface (ice and snow reflect most of the radiation striking that frozen landscape). Through evaporation and heat transfers, the remaining energy radiates back into space. On net, long-lived greenhouse gases—carbon dioxide, methane, and nitrous oxide—contribute about 2.45 W/m^2 to climate change (IPCC 1995d).

At least in part, aerosols (small particles) produced by industry, volcanoes, and other sources can offset an increase in greenhouse gases (Kerr 1995a). Although the particles remain in the atmosphere a relatively short time, while there they do reflect solar energy back into space (IPCC 1995d). After the 1992 volcanic eruption of Mt. Pinatubo, which spewed huge amounts of sulfates into the atmosphere, the world cooled noticeably for several years. Researchers have attributed the failure of the world's temperature to rise as much as predicted to sulfates produced by industry. Aerosol concentrations can make clouds more reflective, thus increasing their cooling effect.

Contentious Issues

Virtually all climatologists agree that an increase in greenhouse gases will affect climate, although they are unsure as to how and to what degree. The theoretical predictions of temperature change have continuously been slashed as more information and better models have been developed. A decade or more ago, researchers forecast sea levels rising 18 feet by the middle of the 21st century; current predictions are more in the range of six inches to three feet in the next 100 years (IPCC 1995d). The 1990 IPCC *Scientific Assessment* forecast global warming at 6° to 14°F by 2050; the 1996 *Assessment* estimated warming of 2° to 6°F by 2100, a cut of more than 50 percent over a period twice as long. In other words, if climate change occurs, it will come at only about one-quarter of the speed of earlier predictions. The IPCC Working Group I concluded (1995d) that the current "best estimate" of temperature warming at the end of the next century would be only 3.6° Fahrenheit, about one-third lower than their prediction five years earlier of 4.5°F warmer for the year 2050.

The speed as well as magnitude of any climate change will determine its effect on the globe. Although many environmentalists have contended that the rate of change in temperature will exceed any that has occurred since the last Ice Age, it now appears that any warming will occur more slowly. Moreover, researchers have now determined that climate variability has been greater over the last 10,000 years than experienced during the last century and a half (Overpeck 1996). The IPCC, however, asserts that over the next century "the average rate of warming would probably be greater than any seen in the last 10,000 years" (1995d). Given that temperatures so far have failed to keep up with model predictions, one can remain skeptical about the future speed of climate change.

An Unknowable Future

Some believe that the warming will be very modest while predicting that a buildup of greenhouse gases will result in increased evaporation and cloud cover. In that scenario, climate change will affect temperature marginally but will have greater impact on rainfall. If that view of warming is correct, any rise in sea levels will be small; the levels may even drop. Accordingly, even though the oceans may warm marginally and thus expand, increased precipitation and especially snowfall in Antarctica will add to the amount of water trapped in glaciers and perhaps lead to a net fall in water levels.

On the other hand, scary news articles have intimated that global warming might melt the polar ice caps and lead to a huge rise in sea levels. Most of the Arctic is covered by ocean with floating ice, which if it melted would not have any effect on water levels. The only large bodies of frozen water that if melted would measurably increase the height of the oceans are located in Greenland and Antarctica. The glaciers in Greenland are surrounded by mountains that block them from sliding suddenly into the sea with potentially large effects. Melting of the Greenland glaciers would take centuries.

The Antarctic is covered with glaciers thousands of feet thick. The West Antarctic ice sheet is open to the sea and thus could potentially be discharged into the sea. Such a development might raise ocean levels by 16 to 20 feet within a hundred years (Bentley 1997). Such a rise would clearly be extraordinarily costly. Fortunately, the experts believe that it is also extremely unlikely. Professor Charles Bentley of the Geophysical and Polar Research Center at the University of Wisconsin writes: "In light of the evidence for recent stability, it is difficult to see how climate warming . . . could trigger a collapse of the WAIS [West Antarctic Ice Sheet] in the next century or two. Ice sheets take thousands of years to respond to changes in surface temperature" (Bentley 1997, 1078).

Not only are we uncertain about the direction of sea levels, but the future growth in greenhouse gas emissions is far from clear. There is little doubt that the concentration of CO_2 in the atmosphere has been rising for well over a hundred years. In 1990, the concentration of carbon dioxide in the atmosphere was measured at 353 parts per million by volume, a rise of 25 percent from the pre-Industrial Revolution figure of 280 parts per million (NRC 1991). Human activity, especially the burning of fossil fuels, has contributed to this

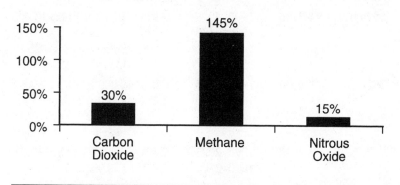

Figure 1-1
GROWTH IN GREENHOUSE GASES SINCE THE
INDUSTRIAL REVOLUTION

SOURCE: IPCC 1995d.

change (see Figure 1-1). What is uncertain is the future. Will humans continue to depend for energy primarily on coal, oil, and the burning of wood? Certainly for the next few decades the world will derive its main source of energy from carbon-based fuels.

In the industrialized West, however, carbon dioxide production relative to national income has been declining (Ausubel 1994). As our economy becomes more information-based and less oriented toward heavy industry, we also become less dependent on coal and petroleum. Predictions about what kind of energy might be used 100 years hence have little validity. Some forecast that, long before then, mankind will have run out of oil and natural gas. Coal supplies appear to be plentiful for several hundred years, but coal has other drawbacks beyond those related to CO_2 emissions. Coal mining is dangerous; burning coal produces sulfur oxides that contribute to acid rain; coal burning also produces particulates that may be hazardous to human health.

The wide range of emission forecasts reflects the uncertainty about future economic growth rates for the world, the availability of cheap fossil fuels, population expansion, and the willingness of countries to pay the costs of cutting emissions. If China were to continue to grow rapidly and to rely on its existing huge stocks of coal, carbon dioxide emissions would continue to grow regardless of whatever

Table 1-3
IPCC ASSUMPTIONS

Scenario	Population in 2100	Period	Economic Growth	Energy Supplies
IS92a,b	11.3 Bil.	1990–2025 1990–2100	2.9% 2.3%	12,000 EJ Oil; 13,000 EJ Gas Solar costs $0.075/ kWh
IS92c	6.4 Bil.	1990–2025 1990–2100	2.0% 1.2%	8,000 EJ Oil; 7,300 EJ Gas; Nuclear costs fall 0.4% yearly.
IS92d	6.4 Bil.	1990–2025 1990–2100	2.7% 2.0%	8,000 EJ Oil; 7,300 EJ Gas; Solar costs $0.065/ kWh; bio available at $50/barrel
IS92e	11.3 Bil.	1990–2025 1990–2100	3.5% 3.0%	18,400 EJ Oil; 13,000 EJ Gas Nuclear phase out by 2075
IS92f	17.6 Bil.	1990–2025 1990–2100	2.9% 2.3%	18,400 EJ Oil; 13,000 EJ Gas Solar costs $0.083/ kWh; nuclear costs $0.09/kWh

SOURCE: IPCC 1992, 11, table 1.

the rest of the world were to do. On the other hand, if there were to be a significant technological breakthrough that reduced the need for reliance on fossil fuels, emissions might even decline. The best guess, however, is that the future path will reflect current rates of economic expansion and current uses of energy sources, and that, while the rate of population growth will be slowing, the number of humans worldwide will still be rising throughout most of the century. The IPCC has established six scenarios, shown in Table 1-3, reflecting differing rates of economic growth, population (projections in billions), and energy supplies in the next century.

Historical Records

The models that employ the various scenarios are poor at replicating past climate and even current weather conditions. Temperature data for the world, measured over the last hundred years, show an increase of about 1°F or less. Partisans point to this as evidence of warming, but much of that boost in worldwide temperatures occurred before 1940 and a good portion took place around 1920, prior to widespread industrialization (Ausubel 1991, 215). From 1940 to the mid-1970s, global temperatures declined a little, setting off speculation about global cooling. Then, starting in the second half of the 1970s, the world became warmer. Overall for this century, temperatures have risen most at night and during the winter with a fall in summer daytime readings (IPCC 1992, 152, table C2).

Within the United States, which has the best records, thermometers have registered no significant gain for the 101 years between 1895 and 1996 (NOAA 1996). Temperatures in 1896 were actually slightly warmer than in 1996! Nor has precipitation varied over the same century. The general circulation models that have been predicting warming forecast that the polar regions should warm the most. Over the last 55 years, no significant warming has been measured at either pole (*World Climate Report* 1995, vol. 1, no. 8). American researchers at the South Pole, who have been keeping records for 40 years, recorded the coldest month ever in July 1997 (Browne 1997, B11).

Moreover, there are real problems with the measurements used to calculate temperature trends worldwide. Those data are based on ground measurements, taken mainly in cities. Most of the world, especially the Southern Hemisphere, is water and there are no figures for much of this area. Mountainous regions also sport few thermometers. Poor and primitive areas are underrepresented in the data since most of the gauges are located in the more economically advanced parts of the world.

Another major problem with the data is that, as cities grow and pave more of their area with asphalt and cement, heat is trapped, thus raising local readings. In other words, the data collected from urban sites are subject to the "heat island" effect. Although climatologists claim to have adjusted for this bias, questions remain about whether the record can accurately portray world temperature changes.

Furthermore, since 1979, satellites circling the earth have measured temperatures around the globe, including much of the world where no one can regularly take temperatures. Those data fail to show an increase in global temperatures over the period 1979 to 1997, even though the models predict and earth-based thermometers show a slight rise. Although the satellite figures are controversial, they are highly correlated with the readings from weather balloons, taken twice a day around the planet (*World Climate Report* 1997, vol. 2, no. 13). Critics of the satellite figures point out that they reflect the average temperature between the earth's surface and 15,000 feet. On the other hand, not only do the data from space cover the planet, but they are free from the heat-island effect and are accurate to within plus or minus 0.02 degrees.

Model Uncertainties

Forecasts of future warming rely not only on the surface temperature data but also on multiequation models run on supercomputers. Using those elaborate models, climatologists have calculated the effect of increases in greenhouse gas emissions on the world's climate. The computer simulations are so big that they require supercomputers to solve the multiple equations. Many factors must simply be assumed. Various parameters are imposed to make the models fit reality. Because of the number of variables involved, weather variables are averaged for very large regions so that they cannot include data on weather fronts, rainfall patterns, or other regional effects (*World Climate Report* 1995, vol. 1, no. 8).

The models replicate current conditions imperfectly. In fact, researchers have had to *adjust* the results to match the models to current weather. As *Science* (Kerr 1994) put it: "In climate modeling, nearly everybody cheats a little." Nevertheless, most of the researchers have concluded that increases in greenhouse emissions will lead to warming of the climate. To nonclimatologists like myself, the predictions may sound reasonable—a buildup of CO_2 and methane will lead to increased retention of heat in the atmosphere. Potential feedbacks, however, might either augment warming or offset it. Professor Richard Lindzen (1994) of the Center for Meteorology and Physical Oceanography at MIT, for example, suggests that negative feedbacks may largely offset the effect of a growth in greenhouse gases. He points out that the standard view assumes a positive feedback effect from water vapor to achieve significant climate change.

Probably the most contentious issue is the effect of clouds on climate. As noted, clouds reflect heat back into space and absorb infrared radiation reflected from the earth's surface. Recent research shows that clouds absorb heat directly from the sun with an unknown effect on climate (*World Climate Report* 1995, vol. 1, no. 7).

In addition the models are singularly poor at predicting regional climate. Until very recently, they also did a poor job of tracking the globe's climate over the last 100 years. They cannot explain, for example, the temperature decline from 1940 to the mid-1970s. Moreover, they predicted that, on the basis of the known buildup of greenhouse gases, the earth's climate should have warmed significantly more than it has.

New modeling has incorporated sulfate aerosols produced by human activity. Those particles reflect solar energy back into space, thus cooling the planet. The significant effect of the sulfate particles was confirmed by the 1991 Mount Pinatubo eruption, which, as noted, threw vast amounts of particles into the upper atmosphere, leading to a measurable cooling of the earth for the next two years. Sulfate aerosols not only reflect energy directly away from the globe but act to condense water vapor into clouds, which also reflect incoming solar radiation away from the earth. The net effect is to reduce the amount of warming from manmade sources. Incorporating the effects of aerosols into the models has led to better predictions of past temperature changes; more important, it has reduced significantly the forecast temperatures and sea level rises resulting from climate changes.

Even when sulfates are included, the computer models fail to track the temperatures in the lower atmosphere (*World Climate Report* 1996, vol. 2, no. 8). Moreover, those portions of the globe with the highest concentration of industry that spews sulfates—Western Europe, Eastern United States, and East Asia—have experienced warming over the last decade and a half, while the rest of the earth has cooled (*World Climate Report* 1996, vol. 1, no. 9). The theory would predict the opposite: the Northern Hemisphere, with most of the world's factories, transportation, oil refineries, and economic activity, should have experienced the least warming rather than the most.

Table 1-4
IPCC SUMMARY

Stabilization Level (CO_2 ppmv)	450	550	650	750
Equivalent CO_2, ppmv	560–760	800–980	920–1160	1140–1340
Cumulative CO_2 Emissions, GtC*	450–620	660–810	760–960	930–1090
Global Mean Temp Change at Equilibrium	2° to 6°	3° to 8°	3° to 10°	4° to 11°

SOURCE: IPCC 1992.
*Gigatons (billions of tons) of carbon.

Table 1-5
IPCC PREDICTED WARMING FOR 2100

Date of Prediction	Best Estimate of Warming
Published in 1990	5.8°F
Published in 1992	4.5°F
Published in 1995	3.6°F

SOURCE: IPCC 1990; IPCC 1995d.

Although the computer models have come up with a range of predictions for increased warming, the current consensus estimates that a doubling of greenhouse gases will boost world temperatures somewhere between 2° and 7°F with a best guess, made in 1992 by the IPCC, a 4.5°F increase. Table 1-4 gives the IPCC's summary of atmospheric concentrations, the total manmade emissions of CO_2, and the predicted mean temperature change.

As noted, the forecasts of climate change have shrunk in recent years as a result of the incorporation of the role of aerosols into the models (see Table 1-5). With somewhat lower temperatures predicted, forecasts of rising sea levels have also fallen. Since climate change is likely to produce more precipitation worldwide, it is likely to contribute to the buildup of ice in Antarctica, which, by itself, should lower sea levels. The warmer oceans will, however, expand. The net result could be either a small fall in the oceans or a rise of perhaps one to three feet by the end of the next century (Schneider 1997). Seashores are rising in some places and falling in others, making it difficult to measure sea level changes accurately; but satellite measurements have failed to find any significant change (Nerem 1997).

Weather Effects of Climate Change

The global warming models predict that the circumpolar vortex, also known as the jet stream, should move toward higher latitudes. The jet stream divides the Northern Hemisphere between the cold polar air and the warmer tropical areas. The winds, driven by differences in temperature, are the major force creating storms and driving precipitation, clouds, and weather fronts. Although a northern movement of the jet stream, especially during the winter, has been expected and would bring warmer weather to much of the hemisphere, the records since 1947 show that the opposite has occurred. The circumpolar vortex has moved farther south, not north as global warming would lead us to expect (Davis and Benkovic 1994).

Many alarmists have suggested that global warming will lead to an increase in the number and severity of storms. Much of the weather that Americans experience is driven by the difference in temperatures between the North Pole and the equatorial region. Since climate change is expected to boost high latitude temperatures more than those near the equator, that temperature differential will be reduced, cutting the differences in atmospheric pressure and thus the severity of most storms. On the other hand, it is true that tropical hurricanes get their strength from warm ocean waters. If global warming occurs, it will expand the area of sea warm enough to generate more hurricanes and perhaps boost the surface temperature of the water itself, possibly making the storms more severe and extending the tropical storm season.

As the next chapter reports, however, warmer periods in the past have experienced less violent storms than colder eras. So far the data for the Atlantic show that violent hurricanes were more common in earlier decades than recently (Landsea et al. 1996). For that region, the number of tropical storms has averaged 9.1 annually since 1960, while the number of such storms in the western Pacific has been 27.5 per year. In that region, no trend is detectable (*World Climate Report* 1996, vol. 1, no. 13). At the same time, the average maximum velocity of sustained winds in Atlantic storms has actually declined since the mid-1940s.

The record of storms over recent decades simply fails to support the proposition that weather is becoming more violent. In the Atlantic basin, the number of intense hurricanes, those scaled between 3 and 5 (5 being the most violent), actually declined during the 1970s and 1980s (Landsea 1993). The four years from 1991 to 1994 enjoyed the fewest hurricanes of any four years over the last half century (Landsea et al. 1996). Researchers have found that the average number of tropical storms and hurricanes has not changed over the past 52 years, while there has been a major *decrease* in the number of intense hurricanes. For the Pacific around Australia, other researchers have found that the number of tropical cyclones has *decreased* sharply since the mid-1980s (Nicholls 1992). Of the 10 deadliest hurricanes to strike the continental United States, all raged before 1960, notwithstanding the huge expansion of population in coastal areas vulnerable to such storms (Landsea 1993).

Environmentalists have viewed climate change as a catastrophe necessitating immediate and major steps to head off or mitigate. Whether global warming will occur is uncertain. Although temperature data until now could reflect a warming planet, they are also consistent with normal fluctuations in weather. From a scientific viewpoint the evidence for global warming must be "not proven."

2. Historical Evidence on Climate and Human Well-Being

> *Climate extremes would trigger meteorological chaos — raging hurricanes such as we have never seen, capable of killing millions of people; uncommonly long, record-breaking heat waves; and profound drought that could drive Africa and the entire Indian subcontinent over the edge into mass starvation. . . . Even if we could stop all greenhouse gas emissions today, we would still be committed to a temperature increase worldwide of two to four degrees Fahrenheit by the middle of the twenty-first century. It would be warmer then than it has been for the past two million years. Unchecked it would match nuclear war in its potential for devastation (Mitchell 1991, 70-71).*
> —former Senate Majority Leader George J. Mitchell

Senator Mitchell's forecast and his history are both wrong. Warmer periods bring benign rather than more violent weather. Milder temperatures will induce more evaporation from oceans and thus more rainfall—where it will fall we cannot be sure, but the earth as a whole should receive greater precipitation. Meteorologists now believe that any rise in sea levels over the next century will be at most a few feet, not 20 (NRC 1991, 24). In addition, Mitchell flunks history: around 6,000 years ago the earth sustained temperatures that were probably more than 4° Fahrenheit hotter than those of the 20th century, yet mankind flourished. The Sahara desert bloomed with plants, and water-loving animals, such as hippopotamuses, wallowed in rivers and lakes. Dense forests carpeted Europe from the Alps to Scandinavia. The Midwest of the United States was somewhat drier than it is today, similar to contemporary western Kansas or eastern Colorado; but Canada enjoyed a warmer climate and more rainfall.

What is well known is that climate changes. The world has shifted from periods that were considerably warmer—during the Mesozoic era when the dinosaurs thrived, the earth appears to have been

23

about 18°F warmer than now—to spells that were substantially colder, such as the Ice Ages when huge glaciers submerged much of the Northern Hemisphere (Levenson 1989, 25). One paleoclimatologist estimated that, during the Precambrian period, the polar regions were about 36°F colder than they are in the contemporary world (Huggett 1991, 74). During the last interglacial era, about 130,000 years ago or about when modern man was first moving out of Africa, the average temperature in Europe was at least 2° to 5°F warmer than at present (Crowley and North 1991, 117). Hippopotamuses, lions, rhinoceroses, and elephants roamed the English countryside. Areas watered today by the monsoons in Africa and east Asia enjoyed even more rainfall then. Indeed during the last 12,000 years (that is, since the end of the last glacial period), the globe has alternated between times substantially warmer and epochs that were noticeably cooler than today's climate.

An examination of the record of the last 12 millennia reveals that mankind prospered during warm periods and suffered during cold ones. Transitions from warm to cold periods or vice versa were difficult for people who lived in climates that were adversely affected yet benefited those who inhabited regions in which the weather improved. On average, however, humans gained during the centuries in which the earth enjoyed higher temperatures. In writing about the effect of climate change on human development, then Senator and now Vice President Al Gore admits:

> The archaeological and anthropological records indicate that each time the ice retreated [during the Ice Ages], the primitive peoples of the Eurasian landmass grew more populous and their culture more advanced. . . . Then, 40,000 years ago, the so-called cultural explosion of tools and jewelry may have coincided with an unusually warm millennium in Europe (Gore 1992, 62-63).

Historical Evidence

History provides the best evidence for the effect of climate change on humans, plants, and animals; but a few researchers have challenged its relevance. David Rind (1993, 39–49), a climate modeler and NASA scientist, has questioned the applicability of past warming episodes to the modern issue of climatic alteration caused by increased CO_2 concentrations. He attributes the origin of past periods of warmth and cold to shifts over time in the orbital position of the earth that impose more or less energy on the poles, as contrasted with a general worldwide warming that might result from the addition of man-made greenhouse gases. He also argues that the swiftness in warming that would occur following increased levels of CO_2 is unprecedented in history. On the latter point, he ignores other research, such as that by a German academic, Burkhard Frenzel, who writes (1993, 7), "During the Holocene [since the last Ice Age], very rapid changes of climate occurred. According to dendroclimatology [tree ring analysis applied to climatology], they often lasted about 20 to 30 years, or [were] even as brief as 2 to 3 years." Other climate historians have found that a rapid cooling in the late glacial period—about 11,000 years ago—took about 100 to 150 years to complete and realized about 5°F variation in temperature within 100 years, more than is being forecast for the next century (Flohn 1983, 404).

Although changes in the earth's orbital position may easily have played a role in warming the earth after the last Ice Age, the effect was worldwide rather than concentrated in northern latitudes. Ice retreated in the Southern as well as in the Northern Hemisphere. Moreover, in the subsequent warming, from around 7,000 to 4,000 years ago, the climate around the world appears to have improved. The evidence for warming in the Southern Hemisphere is weaker but, even if higher temperatures had been localized in one hemisphere or one continent, the effect on human beings would still tell us about the benefits or costs of climatic change. Dr. Rind argues that greenhouse warming would raise winter as well as summer temperatures while past warmings, driven by orbital mechanics, have raised summer temperatures alone. Even though his models suggest that these past warmings should have boosted temperatures solely in June, July, and August, the evidence, albeit a little tenuous for the 3,000-year period of Climatic Optimum, supports warmer winters. For the Little Climate Optimum that coincided with the High Middle Ages, researchers have found strong support for mild winters.

Moreover, at a recent conference the Russians have put forward the hypothesis that past climate changes support the proposition that the cause of the warming or cooling is irrelevant; the pattern has been the same (Broccoli 1994, 282). This conclusion, disputed by some, is based on a large number of past shifts in average weather conditions dating back millions of years. The Russians contend that the climate models overstate the amount of temperature change at the equator and understate it at the poles.

Measurement of Human Well-Being

Since statistics on the human condition are unavailable except for the most recent centuries, I shall use indirect methods to demonstrate the influence of climate on man's well-being. Growth of the population, major construction projects, and a significant expansion in arts and culture all indicate that a society is prosperous. If the population is expanding, food must be plentiful, disease cannot be overwhelming, and living standards must be satisfactory. In addition, if building, art, science, and literature are vigorous, the civilization must be producing enough goods and services to provide a surplus available for such activities. Renaissance Florence was rich; Shakespeare flourished in prosperous London; wealthy Vienna provided a welcome venue for Haydn, Schubert, Mozart, and Beethoven.

Clearly climate is far from the only influence on man's well-being. Governments that extort too much from their people impoverish their countries. A free and open economy stimulates growth and prosperity. War and diseases can be catastrophic. At the same time, a change in climate frequently has been a cause of war or has aided the spread of disease. A shift to more arid conditions, for example, impelled the Mongols to desert their traditional lands to invade richer areas. A cold, wet climate can also confine people to close quarters; confinement can abet contagion. Moreover, a shift toward a poorer climate can lead to hunger and famine, which establish conditions in which disease becomes virulent.

Throughout history climatic changes probably forced technological innovations and adaptations. The shift from warm periods into Ice Ages and back again likely accelerated the evolution of modern man. Each shift would have left small groups of hominids isolated and subject to pressures to adapt to new weather conditions. Those shifts, especially to the more adverse conditions created by the spread of extreme cold, put strong selection pressure on the human forebears that ultimately led to modern man. Even after *Homo sapiens* started spreading across the earth, climate shifts fostered new technologies to deal with changed circumstances.

With the growth in wealth and resources, the influence of climate on human activities has declined. Primitive man and hunter-gatherer tribes were at the mercy of the weather, as are societies that are still almost totally bound to the soil. A series of bad years can be devastating. If, as was the usual case until very recently, transportation is costly and slow, even a regional drought or an excess of rain in one area can lead to disaster, although crops may be plentiful a short distance away. Thus variation in the weather for early man had a more profound influence on life and death than do fluctuations in temperature or rainfall in modern times when economies are more developed. Since the time of the Industrial Revolution, climate has basically been confined to a minor role in human activity.

Climate History

From its beginnings, the earth has experienced periods significantly warmer than the modern world—some epochs have been hotter than the most extreme predictions of global warming—and times much colder than today. Today's cool temperatures are well below average for the globe in its more than 4 billion year history (Giles 1990, 23). During one of the warmest such eras dinosaurs roamed the earth and a rich ecological world flourished.

As mentioned, studies of climate history show that sharp changes in temperatures over brief periods of time have occurred frequently without setting in motion any disastrous feedback systems that would lead either to runaway heating that would cook the earth or freezing that would eliminate all life. In addition, carbon dioxide levels have varied greatly. Ice core data exhibit fluctuating levels of CO_2 that do not correspond to temperature changes (Frenzel 1993, 8). Most past periods display a positive relationship between CO_2 and temperature, however, with a relationship roughly corresponding to that of the Global Climate Models (Crowley 1993, 23). During interglacial periods high latitudes enjoyed temperatures that were about 5° to 11°F warmer than today (Frenzel 1993, 10). Middle latitudes experienced temperatures only about 4° to 5°F warmer. The warmer periods brought more moisture to the Northern Hemisphere, with the exception of central North America during the Holocene. At the time of the medieval warm period, temperatures in Europe, except for the area around the Caspian Sea basin, were

1° to 3°F higher and rainfall was more plentiful than today (Frenzel 1993, 11).

The historical evidence is consistent with only some of the forecasts of the computer climate models. Most climate estimates indicate that a doubling of CO_2 would generate greater rainfall in middle latitudes, and history shows that warm climates do produce more wet weather (Crowley 1993, 21). The historical record shows that land temperatures should increase more than water, thus strengthening monsoons. The models also predict that sea-surface temperatures in the tropics would be higher with increased CO_2, but evidence from the past evinces no such relationship (Crowley 1993, 25).

Carbon dioxide concentrations may have been up to 16 times higher about 60 million years ago without producing runaway greenhouse effects (Rind 1993, 41). Other periods experienced two to four times current levels of CO_2 with some warming. Scientists have been unable to determine whether the warming preceded or followed the rises in carbon dioxide. For virtually all of the period from around 125 million to about 75,000 years ago, CO_2 levels were markedly higher than now.

The prevailing view among climatologists is that the Climatic Optimum—9,000 to 4,000 years ago—resulted from orbital mechanics that increased summer radiation in the Northern Hemisphere, although winters received less heat than they do in the modern world (Webb et al. 1993, 517). Over several millennia, the warmer summers melted the northern glaciers. Warmer lands in the interior of northern continents and cooler oceans drove the monsoons farther north to bring greater rainfall to the Sahara, Arabia, and southern and eastern Asia (Webb et al. 1993, 521). North of the monsoon area, the climate was drier than today. Anatolia, Northwestern Africa, parts of China, and northern Japan experienced less rainfall (Webb et al. 1993, 523). By 4000 B.C., however, a slackening of the trade winds had produced warmer Atlantic ocean water off northwestern Africa; as a consequence, the Middle East, including Greece and modern Turkey, was enjoying more reliable rain.

If orbital variations produced the Climatic Optimum, the Southern Hemisphere should have been cooler. Between 10,000 B.C. and 7,000 B.C., however, winter temperatures (June, July, August) below the equator warmed to levels higher than today while summer temperatures (December, January, February) were cooler than in the modern world (Webb et al. 1993, 525). Rainfall over South America, Australia, and New Zealand was apparently lighter than at present. Although the Southern Hemisphere moved out of the Ice Age in tandem with the Northern Hemisphere, its climate since then has not tracked as closely weather patterns north of the equator (Morley and Dworetzky 1993, 133–34). Data based on vegetation suggest that annual temperatures in New Zealand were coldest between 20,000 and 15,000 years ago, warmed subsequently, and peaked between 10,000 and 8,000 years before the present—somewhat earlier than they did in the Northern Hemisphere (McGlone et al. 1993, 311). Temperatures appear to have been falling over the last 7,500 years. By 1500 B.C., the climate was quite similar to today's (McGlone et al. 1993, 313).

Whether the whole globe warmed or not during the period 7,000 to 4,000 years ago is really irrelevant to the question of how hotter temperatures affect humans. If the Northern Hemisphere warmed, and there is good evidence that it did, then considering how people survived in that portion of the globe provides information about how higher global temperatures would influence mankind.

Modern humans apparently evolved into the current genotype between 40,000 and 200,000 years ago, probably in Africa during an Ice Age (Vigilant et al. 1991, 1503–07). Around 150,000 years ago the extent of ice coverage reached a maximum, followed around 130,000 years before the present (B.P.) by a rapid deglaciation (Crowley and North 1991, 116). The warm interglacial era, during which temperatures may have exceeded those forecast under a doubling of greenhouse gases, lasted about 15,000 years until the onset of renewed glaciation at 115,000 B.P. Over the next 100,000 years the glaciers fluctuated with the climate, but at no time did the average temperature equal the level of the previous interglacial epoch or reach the warmth of the last 10,000 years (Crowley and North 1991, 20).

In the thousands of years of the last Ice Age preceding the current warm epoch, man existed as a hunter-gatherer in a world that looked quite different from today's. Herds of large animals, such as bison, mammoths, and elk, roamed a largely treeless savanna in Europe. Those beasts made easy prey for human hunters who enjoyed as a consequence a rich diet of wild animal meat plus, in season, local fruits and vegetables. It was during the Ice Age that the level of the oceans fell sufficiently to allow Asian peoples to migrate across what is now the Bering Strait but was then dry land. Most archaeologists date the first arrival of humans in the Americas from around 15,000 years ago, although some have claimed evidence for an earlier arrival. No doubt the lower sea levels during the Ice Age also facilitated the arrival of the aborigines in Australia some 35,000 years ago.

Climatologists consider that the last Ice Age ended about 12,000 to 10,000 years ago when the glaciers covering much of North America, Scandinavia, and northern Asia began to retreat to approximately their current positions. In North America the glacial covering lasted longer than in Eurasia because of topographic features that delayed the warming. Indeed, throughout history warming and cooling in different regions of the world have not been exactly correlated because of the influence of oceans, mountains, prevailing winds, and numerous other factors. Nevertheless, across the Northern Hemisphere large temperature shifts have occurred roughly together—perhaps in some areas they have lagged other zones by a century or more. The correspondence between warming and cooling in the Northern Hemisphere and that in the Southern is less well known and, as noted, may be less well correlated because of the predominance of water south of the equator and the existence of Antarctica.

Human progress, a few improvements in hunting tools and some cave art, was incredibly slow during the Ice Age, a period whose length dwarfs the centuries since. Over the last 12 millennia of interglacial warmth, however, modern people have advanced rapidly. The growth in technology and living standards required a climate that was more hospitable than existed throughout that frozen period.

During the last Ice Age humans survived through hunting and gathering. Initially archaeologists believed that those bands, which typically consisted of 15 to 40 people, eked out a precarious existence (Ammerman and Cavalli-Sforza 1984, 4). On the basis of studies of the few bands of hunter-gatherers that survived into the 20th century, however, many modern archaeologists believe that they normally found food plentiful in their forays and would rarely have been hungry. Modern primitive people, however, may not have been typical of earlier groups. The ones that did face food pressures would have adopted farming while those that found ample supplies in their environment would have been less concerned with new ways of acquiring sustenance (Boserup 1981, 39–40). Food pressures could have arisen either from a change in climate that made previous ways of life untenable or an expansion of population in the region that began to overwhelm the natural supply.

As the earth warmed with the waning of the Ice Age, the sea level rose as much as 300 feet; hunters in Europe roamed through modern Norway; agriculture developed in the Middle East. For about 3,000 to 4,000 years the globe enjoyed what historians of climate call the Climatic Optimum period—a time when average world temperatures, at least in the Northern Hemisphere, were significantly hotter than today. At its height, between 4000 and 2000 B.C., the world flourished under temperatures 4° to 5°F higher than have been normal in this century (Lamb 1968, 6). During the relatively short period since the end of glaciation, the climate has experienced what have been described (Wendland and Bryson 1974) as periods of stability separated by "abrupt transition." H. H. Lamb (1968, 12), a leading climate historian, calculates that at its coldest, during the Mini Ice Age (roughly from 1300 to 1800 A.D.), the temperature in central England for January was about 4.5°F colder than it is today. He also concludes that in the central and northern latitudes of Europe during the warmest periods, rainfall may have been 10 to 15 percent greater than now and during the coldest periods of the Mini Ice Age, 5 to 15 percent less (Lamb 1988, 30). On the other hand, cooler periods usually suffered from more swampy conditions because of diminished evaporation.

If modern humans originated more than 100,000 years ago, why did they not develop agriculture for 90 percent of that period? Even if *Homo sapiens* originated only 40,000 years ago, people waited 30,000 years to grow their first crops—an innovation that yielded a more reliable and ample food supply. Farming developed first in the Middle East, right after the end of the last Ice Age—a coincidence? The evidence suggests that, from 11,000 to 9,000 years ago, the climate became warmer and wetter in the Middle East, shifting the ecology from steppe to open woodland (Ammerman and Cavalli-Sforza 1984, 28). This led to the domestication of plants and animals, probably because the warmer, wetter weather made farming possible. From its origins around 8000 B.C., agriculture spread northward, appearing in Greece about 6000 B.C., Hungary 5000 B.C., France 4500

B.C., and Poland 4250 B.C. (Ammerman and Cavalli-Sforza 1984, 41). Is it chance that this northward spread followed a gradual warming of the climate that made agriculture more feasible at higher latitudes?

As anthropologist Mark Cohen (1977, 1) writes, "If, as the archaeological record indicates, hunting and gathering was such a successful mode of adaptation over such a long period of time, and if most human populations are as conservative as anthropologists have observed them to be, we are faced with answering the question why this form of adaptation was ever abandoned." His estimates of the efficiency of the hunting and gathering lifestyle indicate that it was more efficient than farming—at least for large game. He reports that when large animals are available, hunting brings 10,000 to 15,000 calories per hour of hunting. However, if large animals are unavailable—because the environment is poor or because they have all been killed—hunting small game will return only a few hundred to 1,500 calories per hour devoted to that effort. Collecting and processing small seeds from such plants as wild wheat may produce only 700 to 1,300 calories for each hour. Shellfish collection can produce 1,000 to 2,000 calories per hour of work. On the other hand, subsistence farming produces 3,000 to 5,000 calories per hour devoted to agriculture (Cohen 1989, 56). This connotes that hunting large animals, when and if they are available, is the most economical method of subsistence; if the beasts are exterminated or if the humans move to areas without such species, domestication of plants and animals can produce more food for the effort than any other strategy.

Moreover, hunter-gatherers can survive only if the density of their population is low. Too many mouths would strain the environment and preclude survival. Once humans developed farming that could support larger families and a denser population, however, the number of people did explode. Primitive tribes, dependent on hunting, scavenging, and collecting edibles to survive, had to hold their populations below what they might individually have preferred or nature kept them in check through periodic food shortages. A number of 20th-century hunter-gatherers have practiced infanticide and induced abortions to restrict the number and spacing of their children (Boserup 1981, 34). Constant travel by nomads may increase infant mortality and maternal mortality and produce more miscarriages than a sedentary life and thus keep the numbers in check. For primitive peoples, then, farming solved a major problem. Once people settled down into fixed abodes, the population apparently ballooned.

Although many people view the current world's huge population with alarm, most ecologists take the size of the population of a species as an indicator of its fitness. By this criterion, the domestication of plants and animals improved greatly the fitness of *Homo sapiens*. This work is not the place to discuss the capacity of the globe to sustain the number of people expected to populate the world in the next century, but certainly anything that produced greater numbers of people thousands of years ago must have been beneficial for mankind.

Over history the number of humans has been expanding at ever more rapid rates. Around 25,000 years ago, the world's population may have measured only about 3 million (Kremer 1993, 683). Fifteen thousand years later, around 10,000 B.C., the total had grown by one-third to 4 million. It took 5,000 more years to jump one more million; but in the 1,000 years after 5000 B.C., another million were added. Except for a few disastrous periods, the number of men, women, and children has mounted with increasing rapidity. Only in the last few decades of the 20th century has the escalation slowed. Certainly there have been good times when man did better and poor times when people suffered—although in most cases those were regional problems. However, as Figure 2-1 shows, in propitious periods, that is, when the climate was warm, the population swelled faster than during less clement eras.

Figure 2-1 is based on a paper by economist Michael Kremer who argues that, until the Industrial Revolution, existing technology limited the size of the population (Kremer 1993, 681–716). As innovators discovered new techniques and invented new tools, more people could be fed and housed and the population expanded. Moreover, the greater the number of people, the more innovations would be hit upon. He assumed that every individual had an equal but very small probability of uncovering a new technique or device and that the probability of being an innovator was independent of the size of the population. Therefore, the number of inventions would be proportional to the number of people. Thus as the world population expanded—slowly at first—the rate of technological innovation escalated and hence the rate of growth of the population that could be sustained. Only in recent times has technological change become

Figure 2-1
DIFFERENCE IN PERCENTAGE GROWTH RATE OF POPULATION FROM EXPECTED

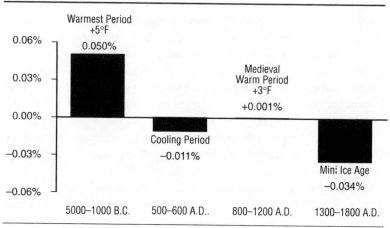

SOURCE: Kremer 1993, table 1; Moore, 1995.

so rapid that it has run ahead of population growth, leading to a rising standard of living, which in turn has reduced the birth rate.

Kremer's hypothesis signifies that for most of history the rate of population growth should be proportional to the size of the population. To link his model and data with climate change, I started with his estimate of the world's people in 10,000 B.C. and calculated the rate of growth of the population over the next 5,000 years. For each subsequent period, I also computed the rate of increase in numbers of people. Comparing the expected rates with actual growth revealed eras in which the number of humans has expanded faster than predicted and periods during which the world's population has grown more slowly. The figure then shows the centuries in which the growth rate of the globe's populace has exceeded or fallen short of the rate expected under this simple model. As can be seen, warm periods have done considerably better than cold periods in human expansion. The warmest period since the end of the last Ice Age produced the highest rate of population growth compared with what would have been expected—in that era agriculture was spreading. Moreover, the Mini Ice Age, which saw the coldest temperatures in the last 10,000 years, underwent the slowest relative population

Figure 2-2
LIFE EXPECTANCY AT VARIOUS PERIODS

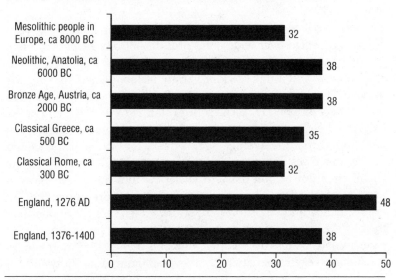

SOURCE: Lamb 1977, 264.

expansion. The figure demonstrates that mankind has prospered in warm periods and the hotter, the better!

Another measure of the well-being of humans is how long they live. The life of the hunter-gatherer was not as rosy as some have contended. Life was short—skeleton remains from before 8000 B.C. show that the average age of death for men was about 33 and that of women, 28 (Boserup 1981, 36–37). Death for men was frequently violent, while many women must have died in childbirth. Since women died so young, they had only around 13 years in which to bear children. Anthropologists have estimated that on average they could have given birth to fewer than five live babies, assuming that they bore a child every 22 months (Boserup 1981, 38). An infant and childhood mortality rate of about 60 percent would have kept the population stagnant.

Figure 2-2 shows some relevant data. People living during the warmest periods—the Neolithic, the Bronze Age, and England in the 13th century—enjoyed the longest life spans of the entire record. The shortening of lives from the late 13th to the late 14th century

35

A.D. with the advent of much cooler weather is particularly notable. Moreover, the rise in life expectancies during the warm period could easily explain the population explosion that took place during that period.

Good childhood nutrition is reflected in taller adults. Skeleton remains collected over wide areas of Eurasia from the period when roving bands shifted from eating large animals and a few plants to smaller prey and a much wider variety of foods attest to a decline in height for both men and women of about five centimeters (two inches) (Cohen 1989, 112). The shorter stature came at the end of the Ice Age when large animals were disappearing. Some archaeologists have found that the average age of death for adults also declined during this transitional period (Cohen 1989, 113). Studies of bone chemistry from Middle Eastern skeletons indicate a reduction in meat consumption. The new diet, although more dependent on grains, fruits, and vegetables, must have been less nutritious than the old. As large game animals disappeared with the end of the Ice Age, humans widened the variety of plants in their diet, increasingly consuming vegetable matter that they had ignored for thousands of years because it was either less nutritious, more difficult to secure and process, or less tasty.

Research on American Indians before the arrival of Europeans also reveals a decline in health between early and later periods (Cohen 1989, 114–15). The evidence for the Americas is more mixed, however, than for Europe. On the basis of Eurasian studies and those of North American aborigines, it seems safe to conclude that health and nutrition were declining *before* the advent of agriculture; it may be that agriculture was invented to stave off further decreases in food availability. The absence of agriculture for most North American peoples may mean that game was more plentiful and their nutrition better than that of their European counterparts.

In southern Europe, the shift to agriculture coincides with a reduction in skeleton size of 3 centimeters (1.2 inches) for men and 4 centimeters (1.6 inches) for women (Cohen 1989, 119). Although some other archaeological studies have found that agriculture led to shorter people, a few have found the reverse. In Israel, for example, one study found that people grew taller with the domestication of animals (Cohen 1989, 119). Overall the evidence supports the view that the diet may have become less nutritious with the shift from

Figure 2-3
AVERAGE HEIGHTS OF ICELANDIC MALES

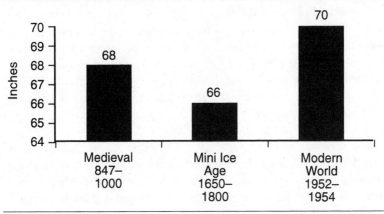

SOURCE: Lamb 1977, 264.

large animal hunting to food production but that its quality initially exceeded that of medieval Europe. Figure 2-3, representing heights, however, signifies that food was more plentiful and better during the medieval period than during the Mini Ice Age.

In summary, the evidence supports overwhelmingly the proposition that during warm periods, humans prospered. They multiplied more rapidly; they lived longer; and they were apparently healthier. We now turn to a closer examination of the two major warm epochs.

The First Climatic Optimum

About 9,000 to 4,000 years ago the earth was much warmer than today; perhaps 4°F hotter, about the average of the various predictions for global warming after a doubling of CO_2 (Lamb 1988, 22). Although the climate cooled a bit after 3000 B.C., it stayed relatively warmer than the modern world until some time after 1000 B.C., when chilly temperatures became more common. During this Climatic Optimum epoch, Europe enjoyed mild winters and warm summers with a storm belt far to the north. Not only was the region less subject to severe storms, but the skies were less cloudy and the days sunnier.

Notwithstanding the less stormy weather, rainfall was more than adequate to produce widespread forests. Western Europe, including parts of Iceland and the Highlands of Scotland, was mantled by great woods (Giles 1990, 133). The timber, until average temperatures dipped temporarily for about 400 years between 3500 B.C. and 3000 B.C., consisted of warmth-demanding trees, such as elms and linden in North America and oak and hazel in Europe. Those species have never regained their once dominant position in Europe and America. Not only did Europe enjoy a benign climate with adequate rainfall, but the Mediterranean littoral, including the Middle East, apparently received considerably more moisture than it does today (Claiborne 1970, 324). The Indian subcontinent and China were also much wetter during this Optimal period (Lamb 1982, 120).

As a senator, Al Gore, writing on the prospect of further global warming and its potential harm, contended that the temperature rise over the last century has led to increased drought in Africa (Gore 1992, 76). To bolster his argument, he presented a chart showing a decline in rainfall from 1930 to the early 1980s for portions of sub-Saharan Africa. His conclusion, however, is based on a false premise: for most of that period the earth was cooling, not warming! His chart actually implies that further cooling would be undesirable. In fact, history demonstrates and climatology attests that warming should drive the monsoon rains that originate near the equator farther north, possibly as far as the Sahara, contributing to a moister, not a drier, climate!

Compared with the cooler periods of the last few thousand years, the Sahara was much wetter and more fertile during the Climatic Optimum (Lamb 1988, 21). Cave paintings from the epoch depict hippopotamuses, elephants, crocodiles, antelopes, and even canoes (Giles 1990, 115–16). The water level in Lake Chad, about 14° north of the equator in central Africa, was some 30 to 40 meters, that is, 90 to 125 feet, higher than it is today, an indication of much greater precipitation. Ruins of ancient irrigation channels in Arabia, probably from the warmest millennia, indicate that they derived their water from sources well above current water supplies, attesting to a wetter climate (Lamb 1977, 270). A warming would likely lead to similar conditions, not a strengthening of African drought. With the cooling that started after 3000 B.C., North Africa dried up and the abundance of life disappeared.

Research has shown, however, that some portions of the globe did suffer from drier conditions. The Caspian Sea may have been at its lowest level in over 80,000 years during the warmest recent period—4,000 to 6,000 years ago—when it was some 20 to 22 meters—66 to 72 feet—below its modern height (Lamb 1977, 130). The Southern Hemisphere seems to have flourished as well during the warm millennia after the most recent Ice Age. Professor Lamb reports that the southern temperate zone enjoyed both warmer weather and more moisture than it does currently (Lamb 1968, 61). Scholars have found that Australia was consistently wetter than today in both the tropical and temperate regions (Lamb 1982, 131). Since the end of that epoch, the great deserts of Australia have expanded and the climate has become both cooler and drier. Apparently most of the other great desert regions of the world enjoyed more rainfall during the Climatic Optimum than they do now. Lamb contends that the period of temperature maximum was also a period of moisture maximum in subtropical and tropical latitudes and a good period for forests in most temperate regions (Lamb 1982, 131). During that warm era, Hawaii experienced more rainfall than in the 20th century (Lamb 1968, 61). Even Antarctica enjoyed warmer weather, about 4° to 5°F higher than at present; during the summer in some of the mountains the weather was warm enough to produce running streams and lakes that have subsequently frozen (Lamb 1968, 62). Nevertheless, the basic ice sheet remained intact.

As already mentioned, the invention of agriculture coincided with the end of the last Ice Age and the melting of the glaciers. Archaeologists have found the earliest evidence for husbandry and farming in Mesopotamia around 9000 B.C. (Claiborne 1970, 243). As the earth warmed, the Middle East became wetter and the Iranian plateau shifted from an open dry plain with roving bands of game to a more wooded environment with less reliable food sources and a diminished supply of large animals. No one really knows how man first domesticated plants and animals; but the coincidence in time and the forcing nature of climate change suggest that the warmer, wetter weather (especially in the mountains) may have encouraged new techniques.

The transition from the Ice Age to a warmer climate that led eventually to agriculture is best documented in Europe. During the cold period, most of Europe was a dry plain, an open savanna, in which large herds of reindeer, mammoths, and bison roamed. As has been shown by the cave drawings in France and Spain, the population secured a good living by preying on those ungulates. As the climate warmed and as rainfall increased, forests spread north, limiting the habitat for the large mammals. Thus humans were forced to follow the dwindling herds northward or develop new sources of food. As the large animals disappeared, the local people shifted to exploiting red deer, wild boar, and smaller species. Those people located near the seas or large rivers found seafood a plentiful source of sustenance. On the other hand, people who made their living at the edge of the ocean faced seas that were rising about 3 feet each century and that often drowned them when high tides and storms washed over their primitive villages.

The domestication of plants appears to have occurred around the world at about the same time: from 10,000 B.P. to 7,500 B.P. (Ammerman and Cavalli-Sforza 1984, 16). The earliest well-documented employment of agriculture arose in the Middle East. Planting of wheat and barley began in southwest Asia between 8000 B.C. and 7000 B.C. In north China's Shensi Province between 4500 B.C. and 3500 B.C., peasants grew foxtail and millet and raised pigs. Food production in that part of China extends back at least into the sixth millennium B.C. In the Americas, domestication of some grains and chili peppers dates from between 7000 B.C. and 6000 B.C.; anthropologists have documented maize in the Tehuacan Valley by 5700 B.C. and production may have started earlier. In South America the evidence suggests that, in the Andean highlands, domestication of two species of beans as well as the chili pepper arose 8,500 years ago. Maize appears in the area only about 3000 B.C. In Africa the evidence implies the cultivation of plants after 3500 B.C. Domestication of cattle occurred in the Sahara about 8,000 years before the present (Ammerman and Cavalli-Sforza 1984, 14–16).

As Professors Ammerman and Cavalli-Sforza put it (1984, 16), "One of the few variables that would seem to be shared is timing: early experiments at plant domestication occurred in southwest Asia, east Asia, and Central America during the period between 8000 B.C. and 5500 B.C." The coincidence of the invention of agriculture with a general warming of the climate, an increase in rainfall, and a rise in carbon dioxide levels, all of which would have made plant growth more vigorous and more plentiful, cannot be accidental.

Domestication of plants and animals represented a fundamental shift in man's involvement with nature. Before that humans simply took what nature offered. People hunted or scavenged the local animals that happened their way. Women gathered fruits and vegetables that grew wild in their territory. With farming and herding, mankind, for the first time, began to modify the environment. Humans determined what would be grown, which plants would survive in their gardens, which animals would be cultivated and bred, and which would be shunned or eliminated. *Homo sapiens* ceased being simply another species that survived by predation coupled with grazing and became a manager of the environment.

The shift from a hunter-gatherer to a sedentary existence may be the most important innovation in human existence. Prior to this change, humans lived in small groups and moved frequently with the seasons to find new sources of meat, fruit, and vegetables. Being mobile meant carrying few goods and only those that were light and not fragile. Thus pottery, which is both heavy and easily breakable, was not part of their culture. Any musical instruments must have been small and portable. Many small children would have been a hindrance as would the elderly and the feeble. Such small groups would have had little opportunity to develop specialization. Virtually all males must have participated in the hunt while all females, not giving birth or caring for infants, must have helped gather edibles. Such tribal or family groups could not have supported elaborate priesthoods, bureaucratic governmental structures, or even people who specialized in artistic, cultural, or intellectual activities. As a consequence, the societies were probably quite egalitarian with only a few, such as the chief or elder and perhaps a medicine man, who stood out from the rest.

The development of agriculture and the establishment of fixed communities led to a population explosion and the founding of cities. Agricultural societies produce enough surplus to support such urban developments, including the evolution of trades and new occupations. A large community could afford to have specialists who made farm tools, crafted pots, and traded within the village and between the locals and outsiders. The people who established the first known city, Jericho, made an early step toward specialization—which lies at the heart of economic advancement—around 8000 B.C. (Lamb 1977, 256).

Farming required the development of property rights in lands, although pastures initially may have been held in common. Even though farm holdings in the beginning were probably fairly equally distributed, over time some families must have acquired larger holdings than others. The increase in income inequality may offend modern sensibilities, but it provided a major benefit. A wealthy class or a rich ruler could afford to maintain individuals who would create desirable objects, such as art, elaborate pots, and musical instruments, and who could record eclipses, star movements, or trade with other centers.

The taming of animals and plants also represents a movement toward establishing property rights. In a hunter-gatherer's world, no one owns the wild beasts or the fruit and grains until they are collected. This can work satisfactorily only as long as demands for the resources are limited. But as the literature on the tragedy of the commons shows, once pressures for more of anything grow too large, the resource base can be exhausted. In what is now called North America, many large species, such as horses, were apparently hunted to extinction. Domestication—privatization of animals and plants—became the answer to overhunting and overgrazing.

In Europe, the Climatic Optimum period produced an expansion of civilization witnessed by the construction of cities and a technological revolution. The Bronze Age replaced the New Stone Age (Lamb 1982, 126). The more benign climate with less severe storms encouraged travel by sea.

During the warm period, trade flourished. People from ancient Denmark shipped amber along the Atlantic coast to the Mediterranean. As early as 2000 B.C., the Celts were apparently sailing from Cornwall and Brittany to both Scandinavia and southern Italy. Astrological monuments built around this time, such as Stonehenge, indicate that the skies were less cloudy than now (Lamb 1977, 254). With the glaciers in the Alps during the late Bronze Age being only about 20 percent of the size of the ice in the 19th century, merchants made their way through the Brenner Pass, the dominant link between northern and southern Europe. Northern Europeans exchanged tin for manufactured bronze from the south. Alpine peoples mined gold and traded it for goods crafted around the Mediterranean. Baltic amber even found its way to Scotland.

During the warm period before 3000 B.C., China experienced much warmer temperatures. Midwinters, in particular, were as much as 9°F hotter and rice was planted a month earlier than is now common

(Lamb 1982, 124). Bamboo, valued for food, building material, writing implements, furniture, and musical instruments, grew much farther north—about 3° in latitude—than is now possible (Ko-chen 1973, 228–29). Chinese archaeologists have found evidence in a district near Sian that the climate 5,000 to 6,000 years ago was warmer and wetter than in the present.

Prior to around 2500 to 1750 B.C., northwestern India, which is now very dry, enjoyed greater rainfall than it does in the 20th century (Lamb 1977, 251). In the Indus Valley, the Harappans created a thriving civilization that reached its apogee during the warmest and wettest periods, when their farmers were growing cereals in what is now a desert (Lamb 1977, 389). The area was well watered with many lakes. That civilization disappeared around 1500 B.C. at a time when the climate became distinctly drier (Claiborne 1970, 295). The earth was cooling. Historians and archaeologists also attribute the failure of the civilization to poor agricultural techniques that may have exacerbated drought.

Virtually all change can make some worse off, and the warming after the last Ice Age is no exception. Although most humans benefited, as the population explosion indicates, the growing warmth harmed some people, especially those who lived near the coast or who had earned their living hunting large animals. As the ice sheets melted, the sea level rose sharply and probably peaked around 2000 B.C. (Lamb 1977, 257, n. 1). During the many centuries in which the waters mounted, storms often led to ocean flooding of coastal communities. A few times each century, people were forced to abandon well-established villages and move to higher ground.

Cooler, More Varied, and Stormy Times

From the end of the Optimum period of sustained warmth until around A.D. 800 to 900, apparently the world's climate, particularly the European, varied between periods of warmth and cold. Based on the height of the upper tree lines in middle latitudes' mountains, temperatures, following the peak warm period around 5000 B.C., demonstrate a more or less steady decline lasting right up to the 20th century (Lamb 1982, 118, fig. 43). Tree ring data for New Zealand indicate that after temperatures reached a maximum around 6000 to 8000 B.C., the climate cooled in that part of the world. (McGlone et al. 1993, 311)

After 1000 B.C. the climate in Europe and the Mediterranean cooled sharply and by 500 B.C. had reached modern average temperatures (Lamb 1988, 22). The period from 500 B.C. to A.D. 600 was one of varied warmth, although cooler on average than the previous 4,500 years. However, the climate became more clement and somewhat more stable from 100 B.C. to A.D. 400, the period of the Roman Empire (Lamb 1988, 23). The Italians grew grapes and olives farther north than they had before that period. During those centuries of varied weather, Classical Greece flourished and then declined; the Roman Empire spread its authority through much of what is now Europe, the Middle East, and North Africa, only to be overrun by barbarians from central Asia whose eruption out of their homeland may have been brought on by a change in the climate.

The cooler climate after the start of the last millennium B.C. appears to have contributed to a southerly migration of people from northern Europe (Lamb 1977, 419). Archaeologists have also found evidence that Greeks adopted warmer clothing after 1300 B.C. The population living in the Alps diminished sharply with the cooler weather, and mining ceased. Classical historian Ray Carpenter (1966) attributes a depopulation of Greece and Turkey between 1200 and 750 B.C. to long-term drought that must have reflected the increased coolness of the climate.

Evidence for a cooler Mediterranean climate from 600 B.C. to 100 B.C. comes from remains of ancient harbors at Naples and in the Adriatic that are located about one meter (three feet) below current water levels (Lamb 1977, 257). Further support for lower sea levels has been found on the North African coast and around the Aegean, the Crimea, and the eastern Mediterranean. Lower oceans imply a colder world, leading to a buildup of snow and ice at the poles and in major mountain glaciers. By A.D. 400, however, temperatures had warmed enough to raise water levels to about three feet above current elevations. The ancient harbors of Rome and Ravenna from the time of the Roman Empire are now located about one kilometer from the sea (Lamb 1977, 258). Evidence exists for a peak in ocean heights in the fourth century A.D. for points as remote as Brazil, Ceylon, Crete, England, and the Netherlands, indicating a world-wide warming.

Changes in the climate in Eurasia appear to have played a major role in the waves of conquering horsemen who rode out of the plains of central Asia into China and Europe. Near the end of the Roman Empire, around A.D. 300, the climate began to warm and conditions in central Asia improved, leading apparently to a population explosion (Claiborne 1970, 344–47). These people, needing room to expand and a way to make a living, invaded the more civilized societies of China and the West. The medieval warmth from around A.D. 1000 to 1300 also seems to have triggered an expansion from that area. During this second optimum period, the homeland of the Khazars centered around the Caspian Sea enjoyed much greater rainfall than earlier or than it does now. The increased prosperity in this area produced a rapidly rising number of young men who provided the manpower for Genghis Khan to invade China and India and to terrorize Russia and the Middle East (Lamb 1977, 250).

After A.D. 550 until around 800, Europe suffered through a colder, wetter, and more stormy period. As the weather became wetter, peat bogs formed in northern areas (Lamb 1968, 63). The population abandoned many lakeside dwellings while mountain passes became choked with ice and snow, making transportation between northern Europe and the south difficult. The Mediterranean littoral and North Africa dried up, although they remained moister than now.

Inhabitants of the British Isles between the 7th and the 9th centuries were often crippled with arthritis while their predecessors during the warmer Bronze Age suffered little from such an affliction. Although some archaeologists have attributed the difficulties of the people during those centuries to harder work, the cold, wet climate between A.D. 600 and 1000 may have fostered such ailments (Lamb 1977, 261).

During the centuries after the fall of the Roman Empire and with the deterioration of the climate, Greece languished. In A.D. 542, the population was decimated by the plague, aggravated by cold, damp conditions; the Black Death struck again between 744 and 747 (Cheetham 1981, 18, 20). As a consequence the number of people was sharply reduced. Greece was partially repopulated in the 9th and 10th centuries when the Byzantine Emperors brought Greek settlers from Asia Minor back into the area. For the first time in centuries Greek commerce and prosperity returned—probably because of an improved climate (Cheetham 1981, 26).

In the 9th century, land hunger and a rising population in Norway and Sweden spurred the Scandinavians to loot and pillage by sea.

Their first descent was on the monastery of Lindisfarne in northern England in 793. That was followed by raids on Seville in Muslim Spain in 844 and later farther into the Mediterranean (Keegan 1993, 288). In the latter half of the 9th century the Scandinavians discovered Iceland and in the next century, Greenland. In 877 they began an invasion of England and conquered from the north to the whole of the Midlands—all of which became a Danish overseas kingdom by the mid-10th century. At the same time, they stormed France and the king had to cede them Normandy as a fief. They also crossed the Baltic (known as Rus in that time) and sent traders south to the Middle East and Byzantium.

The High Middle Ages and Medieval Warmth

From around A.D. 800 to 1200 or 1300, the world warmed considerably and civilization prospered. The period, called the Little Climate Optimum, generally displays, although less distinctly, many of the same characteristics as the first climate optimum (Lamb 1968, 64). Virtually all of northern Europe, Britain, Ireland, Greenland, and Iceland were considerably warmer than at present. The Mediterranean, the Near East, the Arabian peninsula, and North Africa, including the Sahara, received more rainfall than they do today (Lamb 1968, 64–65). North America enjoyed better weather during most of the period. In the early part of that epoch, China experienced higher temperatures and a more clement climate. From Western Europe to China, East Asia, India, and the Americas, mankind flourished as never before.

Evidence for the medieval warming comes from contemporaneous reports on weather conditions, from oxygen isotope measurements taken from the Greenland ice, from upper tree lines in Europe, and from sea level changes. They all point to a more benign, warmer climate with more rainfall; but because of more evaporation, less standing water. Not only did northern Europe enjoy more rainfall but the Mediterranean littoral was wetter. An early 12th-century bridge with 12 arches that still exists over the river Oreto at Palermo exceeds the needs of the small trickle of water that flows there now (Lamb 1968, 8). According to Arab geographers, two rivers in Sicily that are too small for boats today were navigable during that period (Lamb 1977, 271). In England at the same time, medieval water mills on streams that today carry too little water to turn them attest to greater rainfall. Although England apparently received more rainfall than in modern times, the warm weather led to more drying out of the land. Support for a more temperate climate in central Europe comes from the period in which German colonists founded villages. As average temperatures rose, people established towns at higher elevations. Early settlements were under 650 feet in altitude; those from a later period were between 1,000 and 1,300 feet high; those built after 1100 A.D. were located above 1,300 feet (Bartlett 1993, 162).

The great historian of climate, H. H. Lamb, counted manuscript reports of flooding and wet years in Italy (Lamb 1977, 427). He discovered that starting in the latter part of the 10th century, the number of wet years climbed steadily, reaching a peak around 1300 A.D. Over the same period, northern Europe was enjoying warmer and more clement weather. Not only was the temperature higher than now in Europe during the 12th and 13th centuries but the population enjoyed mild, wet winters. In the Mediterranean it was moist as well, with frequent reports of summer thunderstorms (Lamb 1977, 429).

Studies have shown that some areas became drier during those centuries. In particular, the Caspian Sea was apparently four meters—over 13 feet—lower from the 9th through the 11th century than currently (Lamb 1977, 133). After A.D. 1200 the elevation of the sea rose sharply for the next 200 or 300 years ((Lamb 1977, 439). In the Asian steppes, warm periods with fine summers and often with little snow in the winters produced water levels that were low by modern standards (Lamb 1977, 136). A recent study of tree rings from areas as widely distant as California's Sierra Nevada and Patagonia concluded that the "Golden State" endured extreme droughts from around 900 to 1100 and again from 1210 to 1350 A.D., while the tip of South America during the first 200 years also suffered from little precipitation (Stine 1994, 546–49).

The timing of the medieval warm spell, which lasted no more than 300 years, was not synchronous around the globe. For much of North America, for Greenland, and in Russia, the climate was warmer between 950 and 1200 A.D. (Lamb 1977, 435). The warmest period in Europe appears to have come later, roughly between 1150 and 1300 A.D., although parts of the 10th century were quite warm. Evidence from New Zealand indicates peak temperatures from 1200 to 1400 A.D.

Data on the Far East are meager but mixed. Judging from the number of severe winters reported by century in China, the climate was somewhat warmer than normal in the 9th, 10th, and 11th centuries, cold in the 12th and 13th, and very cold in the 14th. Chinese scholar Chu Ko-chen reports that the 8th and 9th centuries were warmer and received more rainfall but that the climate deteriorated significantly in the 12th century (Ko-chen 1973, 235). He found records, however, that show that the first half of the 13th century was quite clement; very cold weather returned in the 14th century (Ko-chen 1973, 237–38). On the basis of records of major floods and droughts, another historian found that between the 9th and 11th centuries China suffered many fewer of these calamities than during the 14th through the 17th (Chao 1986, 203).

The evidence for Japan is based on records of the average April day on which the cherry trees bloomed in the royal gardens in Kyoto. From this record, the 10th century springs were warmer than normal; in the 11th century springs were cooler; the 12th century experienced the latest springs; the 13th century was average and the 14th was again colder than normal (Lamb 1977, 443, 447, tables 17-3,17-4). That record suggests that the Little Climate Optimum began in Asia in the 8th or 9th centuries and continued into the 11th. The warm climate moved west, reaching Russia and central Asia in the 10th through the 11th, and Europe from the 12th to the 14th. Some climatologists have theorized that the Mini Ice Age also started in the Far East in the 12th century and spread westward, reaching Europe in the 14th (Ko-chen 1973, 239–40).

Europe

The warm period coincided with an upsurge of population almost everywhere, but the only numbers are for Europe. For centuries during the cold, damp "Dark Ages," the population of Europe had been relatively stagnant. Towns shrank to a few houses clustered behind city walls. Although we lack census data, the figures from Western Europe after the climate improved show that cities grew in size; new towns were founded; and colonists moved into relatively unpopulated areas.

Historians have failed to agree on why, after the 11th century, the population soared. It may be more enlightening to ask why the population remained stagnant for so long. As John Keegan (1993,

149), the eminent military historian, put it: "The mysterious revival of trade between 1100 and 1300, itself perhaps due to an equally mysterious rise in the European population from about 40,000,000 to about 60,000,000, in turn revived the life of towns, which through the growth of a money economy won the funds to protect themselves from dangers beyond the walls."

Although it is impossible to document, the change in climate from cold and wet to warm and drier—it had more rainfall, but more evaporation reduced bogs and marshy areas—seems likely to have played a significant role. In the 8th through the 11th centuries, most people spent considerable time in dank hovels, avoiding the inclement weather. Those conditions were ripe for the spread of disease. Tuberculosis, malaria, influenza, and pneumonia undoubtedly took many small children and the elderly—those over 30.

Written records confirm that the warmer climate brought drier and consequently healthier conditions to much of Europe. Robert Bartlett (1993, 155) quotes H. E. Hallam in *Settlement and Society* about the people of Holland who invaded Lincolnshire in 1189: "Because their own marshes had dried up, they converted them into good and fertile ploughland." Moreover, before the 12th century German settlers on the east side of the Elbe frequently ended the names of their towns with *mar*, meaning marsh, but later colonists did not use that suffix. Bartlett (1993, 162) explains that the term had gone out of use, but an alternative explanation is that the warmer climate had dried up the marshes.

With a more pleasant climate, people spent longer periods outdoors; food supplies were more reliable. Even the homes of the peasants would have become warmer and less damp. The draining or drying up of marshes and wetlands reduced the breeding grounds for mosquitoes that brought malaria. Overall the infant and childhood mortality rate must have fallen, spawning an explosion in population.

From the 9th century, with a climate still quite cool, to the 11th, medieval Europe was almost totally agricultural. The few cities that existed consisted mainly of religious seats with their support personnel. Even as late as the 12th century, city dwellers made up less than 10 percent of the population (Pirenne, c. 1938, 59). Trade before the 11th century was virtually nonexistent (Pirenne, c. 1938, 12). People were tied to the land through custom and necessity. The great feudal estates grew what they ate and ate what they grew; they wove their own cloth and sewed their own clothes; they built what little furniture was needed. In short, they were almost entirely self-sufficient. The serfs that tilled the land had inherited rights to enough land to sustain a family. Typically the older son would follow his father. Other sons either joined the priesthood or became monks, vagabonds, or in later centuries, mercenaries. Given the cold climate before the 11th century, the lack of medical care, and a restricted diet fostering poor nutrition, few babies lived to adulthood. The problem of an excess of labor was, therefore, nonexistent. In truth the population was growing so slowly that a labor shortage persisted and the feudal nobility established laws prohibiting serfs from leaving their land.

Until the 12th century when the weather became significantly more benign, a Europe fettered by tradition remained cloistered in self-sufficient units. The next two centuries, however, witnessed a profound revolution that, by the end of the 13th century, transformed the landscape into an economy filled with merchants, vibrant towns, and great fairs. Crop failures became less frequent; new territories were brought under control. With a more clement climate and a more reliable food supply, the population mushroomed. Even with the additional arable land permitted by a warmer climate, the expansion in the number of mouths exceeded farm output: food prices rose while real wages fell. Farmers, however, did well with more ground under cultivation and low wages payable to farm hands (Donkin 1973, 90).

Although the first sons born on the estates could follow their fathers, other children, especially the men, had to find new opportunities. The Crusades furnished an occasion for the sons both of serfs and of the nobility to enrich themselves and even to find new land to cultivate. Others moved to virgin territory in eastern Europe, Scandinavia, or previously forested or swampy areas (Bartlett 1993, ch. 6). The Franks and Normans launched invasions of England, southern Italy, Byzantine Greece, and the eastern Mediterranean. In 1130 the Tancred de Hauteville clan, a notable example, founded the Kingdom of Sicily. That family, a classic case of "over-breeding, land-hungry lesser nobility," consisted of 12 sons from two mothers who, recognizing that their Norman property was inadequate, invaded southern Italy in search of land and riches (Bartlett 1993, 48).

During the High Middle Ages, the Germans advanced across the Elbe to take land from pagan Serbs. The spread of knights and soldiers out of France and Germany demonstrates that the population was multiplying more rapidly in northern Europe than in southern. The rapid rise in numbers north of the Alps fits the improved climatic scenario: global or continental warming brought greater temperature change and more beneficial weather to higher latitudes.

The more skilled and enterprising who did not seek their fortune in foreign lands typically flocked to towns and urban centers, becoming laborers, artisans, or traders. Those who moved to the new cities and those who founded colonies were both legally freed of feudal obligations. That new liberty, making risk-taking and innovation possible, was essential for those in commerce.

The warmth of the Little Climate Optimum made territory farther north cultivable. In Scandinavia, Iceland, Scotland, and the high country of England and Wales, farming became common in regions that neither before nor since have yielded crops reliably. In Iceland, oats and barley were cultivated. In Norway, farmers planted farther north and higher up hillsides than at any time for centuries. Greenland savored weather that was 4° to 7°F warmer than at present; settlers could bury their dead in ground that is now permanently frozen. Scotland flourished during the warm period with increased prosperity and construction (Lamb 1977, 437). Greater crop production meant that more people could be fed, and the population of Scandinavia exploded (Claiborne 1970, 348–64). The rapid growth in numbers in turn propelled and sustained the Viking explorations and led to the foundation of colonies in Iceland and Greenland.

The increasingly warm climate was reflected in a rising sea level. People were driven out of the lowlands and there was a large-scale migration of men and women from those areas to places east of the Elbe and into Wales, Ireland, and Scotland. Flemish dikes to hold back the sea date at least from the early 11th century. Although Pirenne and Bartlett attribute them to attempts to reclaim land from the sea to provide new areas for farming, the evidence points toward a climbing water level that farmers in the Low Countries had to battle (Pirenne, c. 1938, 76; Bartlett 1993, 114–15). The earliest texts setting out rights on the reclaimed land fail to mention any obligation to maintain the dikes, although later ones spell out the requirement, suggesting that the problem of holding back the sea became worse over time. Robert Bartlett quotes from a Welsh chronicle on the influx of people from Flanders:

> that folk, as is said, had come from Flanders, their land, which is situated close to the sea of the Britons, because the sea had taken and overwhelmed their land ... after they had failed to find a place to live in—for the sea had overflowed the coast lands, and the mountains [sic] were full of people so that it was not possible for everyone to live together there because of the multitude of the people and the smallness of the land (Bartlett 1993, 115).

In addition to the land north of the Alps, the warmer, rainier climate benefited southern Europe, especially Greece, Sicily, and southern Italy. All of the *Mezzogiorno* in the Middle Ages did well (Cheetham 1981, 37). Nicolas Cheetham, a former British diplomat who wrote a recent book, *Mediaeval Greece*, reports that during the first half of the 13th century, the plains and valleys of the Peloponnese were fertile and planted with a wide variety of valuable crops and trees. They produced wheat, olives, fruit, honey, cochineal for dyeing, flax for the linen industry, and silk from mulberry trees. The wealthy in Constantinople prized highly the wines, olives, and fruit from Greece. Thessaly's grain fed the Byzantine Empire (Cheetham 1981, 28). Patras exported textiles and silk of very high quality. Extensive forests full of game supplied acorns for hordes of pigs. Herders raised sheep and goats in the mountain pastures, while in the valleys farmers kept horses and cattle (Cheetham 1981, 85).

The Mediterranean flourished in the 12th century. Christian and Muslim lands achieved great brilliance. Cordova, Palermo, Constantinople, and Cairo all thrived, engendering great tolerance for contending religions (Cheetham 1981, 35–36). Christian communities survived and prospered in Muslim Cairo and Cordova. The rulers of Byzantium countenanced the followers of Mohammed and often preferred them to "barbaric" Westerners.

In the West, Charlemagne, creator of the Holy Roman Empire, may have inaugurated the era of the High Middle Ages while Dante, writing *The Divine Comedy*, may have closed it. In *A History of Knowledge*, Charles Van Doren (1991, 111) contends that "the ... three centuries, from about 1000 to about 1300, became one of the most optimistic, prosperous, and progressive periods in European history." All across Europe, the population went on an unparalleled

building spree, erecting at huge cost spectacular cathedrals and pub-
lic edifices. Byzantine churches gave way to Romanesque, to be
replaced in the 12th century by Gothic cathedrals. During the period
construction began on the Abbey of Mont-Saint-Michel (1017), St.
Mark in Venice (1043), Westminster Abbey in London (1045), the
Cathedral of our Lady in Coutances (1056), the Leaning Tower at
Pisa (1067), the Cathedral of Santiago de Compostela in northern
Spain (1078), the Cathedral of Modena (1099), Vézélay Abbey in
France (1130), Notre-Dame in Paris (1163), Canterbury in England
(1175), Chartres (1194), Rouen's cathedral in France (1201), Burgos'
cathedral in Castile (1220), the basilica of Saint Francis in Assisi
(1228), the Sainte Chapelle in Paris (1246), Cologne Cathedral (1248),
and the Duomo in Florence (1298). Virtually all the magnificent
religious edifices that we visit in awe today were started by the
optimistic populations of the 11th through the 13th centuries,
although many were not finished for centuries. In southern Spain,
the Moors laid the cornerstone in 1248 for perhaps the world's most
beautiful fortress, the Alhambra. Also in the middle of the 13th
century, the Franks founded a fort, Mistra, near ancient Sparta,
which later became a Byzantine city known for its art and culture.

It took a prosperous society to launch such major architectural
projects. In Europe, building the cathedrals required a large and
largely experienced pool of labor. During the week of June 23 to June
29, 1253, the accounts of the construction at Westminister Abbey, for
example, show 428 men on the job, including 53 stonecutters, 49
monumental masons, 28 carpenters, 14 glassmakers, 4 roofers, and
220 simple laborers (Gimpel 1983, 68, table). Nearly half of all workers were skilled specialists. Even during the slowest season in
November, the Abbey employed 100 workers, including 34 stonecutters. Masons and stonecutters earned the highest wages and usually
hired a number of workers as assistants. Master craftsmen moved
from job to job around Europe without any concern about national
borders—the first truly European Community. Historians have
found that only 5 to 10 percent of the masons and stonecutters
were local people, whereas 85 percent of the men who quarried
the stones—an unhealthy and arduous job—were from the vicinity
(Gimpel 1983, 69).

Economic activity blossomed throughout the Continent. Banking,
insurance, and finance developed; a money economy became well

established; manufacturing of textiles expanded to levels never seen before. Farmers were clearing forests, draining swamps, and expanding food production to new areas (Bartlett 1993, 2). The building spree mentioned was made possible by low wages resulting from a population explosion and by the riches that the new merchant classes were creating. In England, virtually all the churches and chapels that had originally been built of wood were reconstructed in stone between the 12th and 14th centuries (Donkin 1973, 110–11). With the clergy still opposing buying and selling for gain, those who became wealthy often constructed churches or willed their estates or much of them to religious institutions as acts of redemption (Pirenne c. 1938, 50). In that way they supplied much of the funding needed to erect the great Gothic cathedrals.

Starting in the 11th century, European traders developed great fairs that brought together merchants from all over Europe. At their peak in the 13th century, they were located on all the main trade routes and not only served to facilitate the buying and selling of all types of goods but also functioned as major money markets and clearing-houses for financial transactions. The 14th century saw the waning of those enterprises, probably because the weather became so unreliable and poor that transport to and from these locations with great stocks of goods became impractical. Belgian historian Henri Pirenne attributes their decline to war, which may indeed have played a role; but the failure of crops and the increased wetness must have made travel considerably more difficult (Pirenne c. 1938, 103). Wet roads became muddy tracks, rendering the transport of heavy goods arduous. Crop failures made for famines and more vagabonds who preyed on travelers.

During the High Middle Ages of the 12th and 13th centuries, technology grew rapidly. New techniques expanded the use of the water mill, the windmill, and coal for energy and heat. Sailing improved through the invention of the lateen sail, the sternpost rudder, and the compass. Governments constructed roads and contractors developed new techniques for use of stone in construction. New iron-casting techniques led to better tools and weapons. The textile industry began employing wool, linen, cotton, and silk and, in the 13th century, developed the spinning wheel. Soap, an essential for hygiene, came into use in the 12th century. Mining, which had declined since the Romans, at least partly because the cold and snow made access to mountain areas difficult, revived after the 10th century.

Farmers and peasants in medieval England launched a thriving wine industry south of Manchester. Good wines demand warm springs free of frosts, substantial summer warmth and sunshine without too much rain, and sunny days in the fall. Winters cannot be too cold—not below zero Fahrenheit for any significant period. The northern limit for grapes during the Middle Ages was about 300 miles above the current commercial wine areas in France and Germany. The wines were not simply marginal supplies but of sufficient quality and quantity that, after the Norman conquest, the French monarchy tried to prohibit British wine production (Lamb 1977, 277). From average and extreme temperatures in the most northern current wine-growing regions of France and Germany compared with current temperatures in the former wine-growing regions in England, Lamb calculates that the temperature in spring and summer was somewhere between 0.9° and 3.4°F warmer in the Middle Ages (1977, 278–79).

Not only did the British produce wines during the Little Climate Optimum but farmers grew grapes in East Prussia, Tilsit, and south Norway (Lamb 1977, 279). Many areas cultivated in Europe were much farther up mountains than is possible under the modern climate. Together those factors suggest that the temperatures in central Europe were about 1.8° to 2.5°F higher than during the 20th century.

Europe's riches and a surplus of labor enabled and emboldened its rulers to take on the conquest of the Holy Land through a series of Crusades starting in 1096 and ending in 1291 A.D. The Crusades, stimulated at least in part by a mushrooming population and an economic surplus large enough to spare men to invade the then Muslim empire, captured Jerusalem in 1099—a feat not equaled until the 19th century. A major attraction of the first Crusade was the promise of land in a "southern climate" (Keegan 1993, 291).

Even southern Europe around the Mediterranean enjoyed a more moist climate than currently (Lamb 1968, 8). In the reign of the Byzantine emperor Manuel I Comnenus, art and culture flourished and all the world looked to Constantinople as its leader (Langer 1968, 269). Under the control of the Fatimid caliphate, Egypt cultivated a "House of Science" where scholars worked on optics, compiled an encyclopedia of natural history, with a depiction of the first known windmills, and described the circulation of the blood. In Egypt, block-printing appeared for the first time in the West (Langer 1968,

206, 286). The caliphate turned Cairo into a brilliant center of Islamic culture. In Persia (today's Iran), Omar Khayyam published astronomical tables, a revision of the Muslim calendar, a treatise on algebra, and his famous *Rubáiyát* (Carruth 1993, 161).

As European commerce expanded, traders reached the Middle East, bringing back not only exotic goods but new ideas and information about classical times. Drawing on fresh information about Aristotelian logic, St. Thomas Aquinas defined medieval Christian doctrine in his *Summa Theologica*. Possibly the oldest continuous university in the world was founded in Bologna in A.D. 1000 for the study of the law. Early in the 12th century a group of scholars, under a license granted by the chancellor of Notre-Dame, began to teach logic, thus inaugurating the University of Paris. Cambridge University traces its foundation to 1209 and Oxford to slightly later in the 13th century. Roger Bacon, one of the first to put forward the importance of experimentation and careful research, studied and taught at Oxford in the 13th century.

Secular writing began to appear throughout northern Europe. In the 12th century the medieval epic of chivalry, the *Chanson de Roland*, was put into writing. Between 1200 and 1220 an anonymous French poet composed the delightful and optimistic masterpiece *Aucassin et Nicolette*. An anonymous Austrian wrote in Middle High German the *Nibelungenlied* (Carruth 1993, 134, 170, 171).

The Arctic

From the 9th through the 13th centuries agriculture spread into northern Europe and Russia where it had been too cold to produce food before. In the Far East, Chinese and Japanese farmers migrated north into Manchuria, the Amur Valley, and northern Japan (McNeill 1963, 559). As mentioned, the Vikings founded colonies in Iceland and Greenland, a region that may have been more green than historians have claimed. It was also during this period that Scandinavian seafarers discovered "Vinland"—somewhere along the East Coast of North America. The subsequent Mini Ice Age cut off the colonies in Greenland from Europe, and they eventually died off. Even today, during this warm period of the late 20th century, the British climate forecloses large-scale grape production and Greenland is unsuitable for farming.

The Eskimos apparently expanded throughout the Arctic area during the medieval warm epoch (Lamb 1977, 248). Starting with

Ellesmere Land around A.D. 900, Eskimo bands and their culture spread from the Bering Sea into the Siberian Arctic. Two centuries later, they migrated along the coast of Alaska and into Greenland. During that period the Eskimos' main means of livelihood was whaling, which had to be abandoned with the subsequent cooling. The Mini Ice Age forced the Thule Eskimos south out of northern Alaska and Greenland. Those hardy aborigines had abandoned Ellesmere Land by the 16th century.

At the same time that the Eskimos were moving north, Viking explorers were venturing into Greenland, Vinland, and even the Canadian Arctic. Scandinavian sailors found Iceland in 860, Greenland around 930, and North America by 986 (Lamb 1977, 252). By the turn of the millennium, when the waters southwest of Greenland may have been at least 7°F warmer than now, Vikings were regularly visiting Vinland for timber (Lamb 1988, 159). They were received with great hostility by the natives and eventually abandoned contact, although the last trip may have occurred as late as 1347, when a Greenland ship was blown off course (Lamb 1977, 252). At the height of the warm period, Greenlanders were growing corn and a few cultivated grain.

The Far East

As noted above, the warming in the Far East seems to have preceded that in Europe by about two centuries. Chinese economist Kang Chao has studied the economic performance of China since 200 B.C. In his careful investigation, he discovers that real earnings rose from the Han period (206 B.C. to A.D. 220) to a peak during the Northern Sung Dynasty (A.D. 961 to 1127) (Chao 1986, 219). This coincides with other evidence of longer growing seasons and a warmer climate. He explains the fall in worker productivity after the 12th century as stemming from population pressures, but a change in climate may have played a significant role. Chao reports that the number of major floods averaged fewer than four per century in the warm period of the 9th through the 11th centuries while the average number was more than double that figure in the 14th through the 17th centuries of the Mini Ice Age (Chao 1986, 203). Not only floods but droughts were less common during the warm period. The era of benign climate sustained about three major droughts per century while during the later cold period, China suffered from almost 13 each 100 years.

The wealth of the period gave rise to a great flowering of art, writing, and science. The Little Climate Optimum witnessed the highest rate of technological advance in Chinese history. During the 300 years of the Sung Dynasty, farmers invented 35 major agricultural implements—that is, over 11 per century, a significantly higher rate of invention than in any other era (Chao 1986, 195). In the middle of the 11th century A.D., the Chinese became the first to employ movable type (Carruth 1993, 151).

During the Northern Sung Dynasty Chinese landscape painting with its exquisite detail and color reached its apogee (Langer 1968, 366). Adam Kesseler, curator of the Los Angeles County Museum of Natural History, dates the earliest Chinese blue-and-white porcelain to the 12th century (Kesseler 1994, A17). The Southern Sung produced pottery and porcelains unequaled in subtlety and sophistication. Literature, history, and scholarship flourished as well. Scholars prepared two great encyclopedias, compiled a history of China, and composed essays and poems. Mathematicians developed the properties of the circle. Astronomers devised a number of technological improvements to increase the accuracy of measuring the stars and the year (Langer 1968, 367).

Japan also prospered during the Little Climate Optimum. In the Heian Period (A.D. 794 to 1192) the arts thrived as emperors and empresses commissioned vast numbers of Buddhist temples. Murasaki Shikibu, perhaps the world's first female novelist, composed Japan's most famous book, The Tale of Genji. Other classical writers penned essays: Sei Shonagon, another lady of the court, wrote Makura-no-Soshi (the Pillow Book). The Japanese aristocracy vied in composing the best poems. All of this attests a prosperous economy with ample food stocks to support a leisured and cultivated upper class.

Over the 400 years between A.D. 800 and 1200, the peoples of the Indian subcontinent prospered as well. Society was rich enough to produce colossal and impressive temples, beautiful sculpture, and elaborate carvings, many of which survive to this day (McNeill 1963, 559). The Lingaraja Temple, one of the finest Hindu shrines, as well as the Shiva Temple date from this period (Carruth 1993, 151). Seafaring empires existed in Java and Sumatra, which reached its height around 1180. Ninth century Java erected the vast stupa of Borobudur; other temples—the Medut, Pawon, Kelasan, and Prambanan—originated in this era. In the early 12th century, the predecessors of the Cambodians, the Khmers, built the magnificent temple of Angkor Wat (Langer

1968, 372). In the 11th century Burmese civilization reached a pinnacle. In or around its capital, Pagan, between 931 and 1284, succeeding kings competed in constructing vast numbers of sacred monuments and even a library (Deland 1987, 9, 29–32). Today the area is a dusty plain littered with the crumbling remains of about 13,000 temples and pagodas built in a more hospitable era.

Archaeologists studying the composition of forests in New Zealand have found that the South Island enjoyed a warmer climate between A.D. 700 and 1400, about the time that Polynesians were colonizing the South Pacific Islands and the Maoris were settling in New Zealand (Lamb 1977, 430–31). Partially confirming that warming are data from Tasmania of tree rings that show a warm period from A.D. 940 to 1000 and another from 1100 to 1190 (Cook et al. 1991, 1267).

The Americas

Less is known about civilizations in the Americas during the Little Climate Optimum or even how the prevailing weather changed. Many of the currently arid areas of North America were apparently wetter during that epoch. The Great Plains east of the Rocky Mountains, the upper Mississippi Valley, and the Southwest received more rainfall between A.D. 800 and 1200 than they do now (Lamb 1988, 42). Radiocarbon dating of tree rings indicates that warmth extended from New Mexico to northern Canada. In Canada, forests extended about 60 miles north of their current limit (Lamb 1988, 42).

Starting around A.D. 800 to 900, the indigenous peoples of North America extended their agriculture northward up the Mississippi, Missouri, and Illinois river basins. By 1000 they were farming in southwestern and western Wisconsin and eastern Minnesota (Lamb 1977, 249). They grew corn in northwestern Iowa prior to 1200 in an area that is now marginal for rainfall (Lamb 1982, 177). When colder, drier weather set in after 1150 to 1200 A.D., Indian settlements on the northern plains of Iowa were abandoned. After that time, the natives substituted bison hunting for growing crops. In general, the land east of the Rocky Mountains enjoyed wetter conditions from 700 to 1200 A.D. and then turned drier as colder Arctic weather intruded more frequently.

The Anasazi civilization of Mesa Verde flourished during the warm period, but the cooling of the climate around 1280 A.D., at the end of the medieval warmth, probably led to its disappearance (Gore 1992, 78). That climatic shift brought drier conditions to much of the region, leading to a retreat from the territory and forcing the Pueblo Indians to shift their farming to the edge of the Rio Grande. Around 900, the Chimu Indians in South America developed an extensive irrigation system on Peru's coast to feed their capital of between 100,000 to 200,000 souls, a huge number for the era (Carruth 1993, 142–43). The Toltec civilization, which occupied much of Mexico, reached its apogee in the 13th century (Langer 1968, 386). By 1200, the Aztecs had built the pyramid of Quetzalcoatl near modern Mexico City (Carruth 1993, 168). The Mayan civilization, however, reached a peak somewhat earlier, before 1000, and declined subsequently for reasons that remain unclear. It is possible that the warming after 1000 led to additional rainfall in the Yucatán, making the jungle too vigorous to restrain and causing a decline in farming, while at the same time improving agricultural conditions in the Mexican highlands and farther north into what is now the southwestern United States.

Thus warmer times brought benefits to most people and most regions, but not all. As is always the case with a climatic shift, the changes benefited some while affecting other adversely. Change is disruptive; at the same time it produces new ideas and new ways of coping with the world. Nevertheless, for most of the known globe, the Little Climate Optimum of the 9th through the 13th centuries brought significant benefits to the local populations. Compared with the subsequent cooling, it was nirvana.

The Mini Ice Age

The Little Ice Age is even less well defined than the medieval warm period. Climatologists are generally agreed that, at least in Europe, North America, New Zealand, and Greenland, temperatures fell, although with many ups and downs, after 1300 to around 1800 or 1850 A.D., when they began to rebound. There was a cold period in the first decade of the 14th century, another around 1430 and yet again in 1560. The end of that period of increasingly harsh temperatures could have been as early as 1700, 1850, or even as late as 1900 A.D. for Tasmania. The worst period for most of the world occurred between 1550 and 1700 (Lamb 1977, 463). One reasonable interpretation of the data is that the world has been cooling since around 4500 B.C. with a temporary upswing during the High Middle Ages.

Europe and Asia cooled substantially from around 1300 to 1850, especially after 1400, with temperatures falling some 2° to 4°F below those of the 20th century. That indicates that temperatures may have dipped by as much as 9°F in the 200 years from 1200 to 1400, a drop of about the same magnitude as the maximum rise forecast from a doubling of CO_2. Those frigid times did bring hardships; and, as Figure 2-1 shows, world population growth slowed. For much of those centuries, famine and disease stalked Europe and Asia.

Glaciers in North America and northern Europe peaked between the late 1600s and 1730 to 1780. In the Alps the ice sheets reached their maximum between 1600 and 1650 A.D. The cold came later below the equator where the glaciers reached their extreme between 1820 and 1850 (Lamb 1988, 166).

Oxygen isotope ratios from oak trees in Germany document a steady decline in average temperatures from 1350 to about 1800, with the exception of a few small upsurges and one strong temperature spike in the first half of the 18th century (Lamb 1977, 450, fig. 17-12). They also confirm a recovery beginning late in the 19th century to much higher levels. Icelandic records of sea ice attest to an increase between 1200 and the middle of the 14th century and then, starting in the latter half of the 16th century, a marked upswing in ice that appears to have peaked around 1800 (Lamb 1977, 452, fig. 17-13). As H. H. Lamb (1977, 461–62) points out, "In most parts of the world the extent of snow and ice on land and sea seems to have attained a maximum as great as, or in most cases greater than, at any time since the last major Ice Age."

The Mini Ice Age, especially the century and a half between 1550 and 1700—the exact timing varied around the globe—produced low temperatures throughout the year and considerable variation in weather from year to year and from decade to decade. It included some years that were exceptionally warm (Lamb 1977, 465–66). The polar cap expanded, as did the circumpolar vortex, driving storms and the weather to lower latitudes. Although much of Europe experienced greater wetness than during the earlier warm epoch, it was more the product of less evaporation due to the cold than of excessive precipitation.

The cooling after the High Middle Ages can be seen in the lowering of tree lines in the mountains of Europe, changes in oxygen isotope

61

measurement, and advances of the glaciers and of sea ice. That cooling diminished the abundance and quality of wine production in France, Germany, and Luxembourg as depicted in historical documents, such as weather diaries and farm records (Lamb 1977, 246). The ocean, which had reached relatively high levels both in the late Roman period and again during the High Middle Ages, fell to lower elevations in the 17th and 19th centuries (Lamb 1977, 432). As a result of an expanded ice cap, the circumpolar vortex, which funnels weather around the globe, moved south and spawned increasingly cold and stormy weather in middle latitudes. With the exception of the southern United States and central Asia, both of which enjoyed more rainfall, this brought a worsening of the climate and disasters to people almost everywhere. During the coldest period of the 17th century, snow fell above 10,000 feet in the high mountains of Ethiopia that today never see snow. The subtropical monsoon rains decreased and receded farther south, causing droughts in East Asia and parts of Africa (Fairbridge 1984, 181–90).

The expansion of the circumpolar vortex produced some of the greatest windstorms ever recorded in Europe and, not so incidentally, changed history. A terrible tempest destroyed the Spanish Armada in 1588. Fierce gales wracked Europe in December 1703 and on Christmas Day 1717 (Lamb 1988, 158). The contrast between the cold northern temperatures that moved south and the warm subtropical Atlantic undoubtedly generated a fierce jet stream. Although we lack any information, that may also have enhanced tornado activity on the plains of the United States (Lamb 1977, 467).

The reduced temperatures had the following general effects: Arctic sea ice expanded in the Atlantic, eventually cutting off Greenland; glaciers advanced in Iceland, Norway, Greenland, and the Alps; the upper tree line in North America and central Europe lowered; enhanced wetness spawned bogs, marshes, lakes, and floods; rivers and lakes froze more frequently; the number and strength of storms, some of which were extraordinarily destructive, intensified sharply; harvests failed, engendering famine and higher prices for basic foods; peasants abandoned farms that no longer enjoyed reliable weather; and disease for both animals and humans spread (Lamb 1977, 451–52).

As early as 1250, floating ice from the East Greenland ice cap was hindering navigation between Iceland and Greenland (Lamb 1988,

159). Over the next century and a half, the prevalence of icebergs became worse. By 1410 sea travel between the two outposts of Scandinavia ceased. Based on the ratio of isotopes of oxygen in the teeth of ancient Norsemen, researchers have estimated that the climate in Greenland cooled by about 3°F between 1100 and 1450 (Monastersky 1994, 310). For about 350 years, from the third quarter of the 15th century to 1822, no ships found their way to Greenland and the local population perished (Lamb 1988, 159).

Harvest failures in the last quarter of the 13th century heralded the deteriorating climate in Europe. Compounding the insufficiency was a shift of land from farming—which, because of the change in climate, was more chancy—to enclosure and sheep rearing (Lamb 1977, 7). Average yields, already low by modern standards, worsened after the middle of the 13th century (Donkin 1973, 91). One of the first severe bouts of cold wet weather afflicted Europe from 1310 to 1319, leading to large-scale crop failures (Lamb 1977, 454). Food supplies deteriorated sharply, generating famine for much of Europe in 1315–18 and again in 1321 (Donkin 1973, 90). Harvest deficits and hunger preceded the Black Death by 40 years (Lamb 1977, 266). According to Lamb (1977, 7), in much of the Continent, "the poor were reduced to eating dogs, cats and even children." That scanty food output contributed to a decline in population that was aggravated by disease. The history of many villages shows that they were abandoned before, not after, the beginning of the plague. By 1327, the population in parts of England—especially those later devastated by the plague—had fallen by 67 percent (Lamb 1977, 454). People poorly nourished were quickly carried off by disease. Between 1693 and 1700 in Scotland, seven of the eight harvests failed and a larger percentage of the population starved than had died in the Black Death of 1348–50 (Lamb 1977, 471).

In two terrible years, 1347 and 1348, famine struck northern Italy, followed by the Black Death, which decimated most of those not already carried away by lack of food (Langer 1968, 317). Bubonic plague spread across the Alps after 1348, killing in the next two years about one-third of northern Europe's people. Life expectancy fell by 10 years in a little over a century, from 48 years in 1280 to 38 years in the years 1376 to 1400 (Lamb 1982, 189). Crops often failed; peasants abandoned many lands that had been cultivated during the earlier warm epoch. Between 1300 and 1600, the growing season shrank by three to five weeks with a catastrophic impact on farming (Lamb 1988, 32). In Norway and Scotland, the population declined and villagers deserted many locales well before the plague reached those areas (Lamb 1988, 36). The capitals of both Scotland and Norway moved south before both areas lost their autonomy.

The cooling after 1300 probably contributed significantly to the virulence of the bubonic plague, the greatest disaster ever to befall Europe. The disease appears to have originated around 1333 in China, shortly after major rains and floods in 1332, which are reputed to have caused 7 million deaths while disturbing wildlife and displacing plague-carrying rats (Lamb 1977, 456). Around 1338–39, the Black Death spread to central Asia, which, with the increased coldness, was also drying out. By 1348 rodents carrying fleas infested with bubonic plague had marched or been carried from the Crimea into Europe. Historians have estimated that as many as one-third of all the people in Europe died in the raging epidemic that swept the Continent (Lamb 1977, 262). That outburst of the plague, like a similar one in the 6th century, occurred during a period of increasing coolness, storminess, and wet periods, followed by dry, hot ones. The unpleasant weather is likely to have confined people to their homes where they were more likely to be exposed to the fleas that carried the disease. In addition, the inclement weather may have induced rats to take shelter in buildings, exposing their inhabitants to the bacillus.

Not only did the cold facilitate the spread of the plague, but it caused much other human suffering. Several centuries later, in July 1789, just before the French Revolution, wet weather and air temperatures between 59 and 85°F produced an ergot blight in the rye crop of Brittany and other parts of France. The blight induced hallucinations, paralysis, abortions, and convulsions and came after a very cold winter that had created severe food shortages (Lamb 1988, 165). Earlier in that century wet, cold summers had brought about two years of famine in Europe.

The end of the medieval warmth had devastating effects on populations that lived at the edge of habitable lands. Historians, for example, have estimated the population of Iceland in the last decades of the 11th century at about 77,000; and early in the 14th it still numbered over 72,000. By 1800, after several hundred years of coolness and stormy weather, the poor conditions had more than halved, to 38,000, the number of Icelanders (Lamb 1977, 265; from Thorarinsson 1961).

The terrible climate in Europe after the 13th century brought a halt to the economic boom of the High Middle Ages. Innovation slowed sharply (Gimpel 1983, 150). Except for military advances, technological improvements ceased for the next 150 years. Population growth not only ended but, with starvation and the Black Death, fell. Without the drive of additional numbers of people, colonial enterprise ceased and no new lands were reclaimed nor towns founded. The economic slump of 1337 brought on the collapse of the great Italian bank, Scali, leading to one of the first recorded major financial crises (Gimpel 1983, 151). Construction halted on churches and cathedrals.

The hardships of the 14th century induced a search for scapegoats. In 1290, after some years of crop failures, the king of England expelled the entire Jewish population from the country. The French king followed that example in 1306 and again in 1393 (Pirenne c. 1938, 134). In 1349, the Christians of Brabant massacred local Jews; they expelled the remainder 21 years later.

The Mini Ice Age at its coldest devastated the fishing industry. From 1570 to 1640, during the most severe period, Icelandic documents record an exceptionally high number of weeks with coastal sea ice. Between 1615 and 1828, with the exception of a few years, fishermen from the Faeroe Islands suffered from a lack of cod—cod needs water warmer than 36°F to flourish. During the worst period, 1685 to 1704, fishing off southwest Iceland failed totally (Lamb 1988, 153–54, 155). In the very icy year of 1695, Norwegian fishermen found no cod off their coast. Lamb calculates that the sea around the Faeroe Islands was probably 7° to 9°F colder than it had been over the last century (1988, 156, 160).

The Mini Ice Age brought hard times to southern Europe as well. Severe winters and wet summers created shortages and famines in the south of France and in Spain. The great variability in the weather made agricultural output uncertain and contributed to a farming crisis in the Iberian Peninsula. Although there were certainly other causes as well, it seems very likely that the deterioration in climate contributed greatly to the economic decline of the Mediterranean littoral in the 17th century (Lamb 1977, 469).

The cold had devastating effects elsewhere in the world. Between 1646 and 1676, frosts killed the orange trees in the Chinese province of Kiangsi (Lamb 1977, 471). As food prices rose, per capita incomes fell. As already mentioned, cooler weather brought an end to the Anasazi Indian pueblo culture and to native American farming in the upper Midwest.

According to Nicolas Cheetham, in the second half of the 13th century, warfare in Greece and the necessity of keeping a large military establishment under arms reduced the country's previous prosperity. War does exact a high toll on economies, but it seems extraordinarily coincidental that economic troubles occurred at the time Europe was experiencing a deteriorating climate. In 1268, the king of Naples, in gratitude for military service, sent wheat, barley, and cattle to the Peloponnese to relieve the hunger caused by crop failures (Cheetham 1981, 98–99). Were the crop failures caused solely by military disruptions? Although his death was not necessarily weather related, in 1275 Geoffroy de Briel, a major figure in medieval Greece, died during a military campaign of dysentery, a disease often exacerbated by cold, wet conditions (Cheetham 1981, 101).

Notwithstanding the cooling climate and the ravages of disease after 1300, European civilization recovered in the 15th century with the advent of the Renaissance. This burst of cultural activity represented a continuation, an expansion, and a deepening of the artistic and intellectual activity of the High Middle Ages. Ironically, the plague may have established the conditions necessary for the outpouring of art, science, and literature that made up the Renaissance. The colder climate made agriculture more chancy, reduced the territory available for farming, and cut yields. Yet without the one-third drop in Europe's population caused by the Black Death, food supplies would have been too meager to support a large artistic and cultured class that promoted and supported the arts. The reduced agricultural output, however, was still large enough to support the even more diminished population. In China, which experienced a slower decline in numbers, real wages fell and the people became increasingly impoverished (Kremer 1993, 714, app. A; Chao 1986, 218, table 9-2). But in Europe, as a result of such a terrible death rate over a short period, real incomes for the survivors actually climbed (Rosenberg and Birdzell Jr. 1986, 54).

From roughly 1550 to 1700, the globe suffered from the coldest temperatures since the last Ice Age. Lamb estimates that in the 1590s and 1690s the average temperature was 3°F below the present. Grain prices increased sharply as crops failed. Famines were common. The Renaissance had ended; Europe was in turmoil. The Continent suffered from cold and rain, which produced poor growing conditions, food shortages, famines, and finally riots in the years 1527–29, 1590–97, and the 1640s. The shortages between 1690 and 1700 killed millions; they were followed by more famines in 1725 and 1816 (Ladurie 1971, 64–79).

China, Japan, and the Indian subcontinent were also afflicted with severe winters between 1500 and 1850–80. Despite the development of a new type of rice that permitted the cultivation of three crops a year on the same land—up from two—the population of China, as well as that of Korea and the Near East, declined for two centuries after 1200, undoubtedly reflecting a deteriorating climate (Carruth 1993, 166, 168).

Happiness Is a Warm Planet

History has shown us that warm periods are significantly better than cold periods. During the best of times, human populations have gone up rapidly, new techniques and practices have developed, and building and art have flourished. The record shows that human beings spent hundreds of thousands of years as hunter-gatherers, living like many other mammals. Only when the weather warmed did our ancestors domesticate plants and animals and cease scavenging from the land and begin to shape the environment. During the Climatic Optimum of 3,000 to 8,000 years ago, people built the first cities and established city states and then empires. During that period, trade flourished, writing was invented, and the human population exploded. The warmer weather was accompanied by more plentiful rainfall, especially in North Africa and Arabia. Hardwood forests flourished throughout northern Europe.

The climate turned somewhat cooler about 1000 B.C. but was interspersed with some periods of warmth until around 600 A.D. For the next 300 years, the weather was cold and damp, not because of rainfall but from lack of evaporation. In Europe, progress, civilization, and trade came to a standstill.

From 900 to 1300 A.D., especially after the start of the new millennium, warm, sunny weather returned and the population exploded. Traders developed great fairs throughout Europe. Lured by better

weather, people colonized new regions, especially at higher elevations and farther north. The Norsemen occupied Iceland and Greenland and apparently explored the northern reaches of North
America. Europeans went on a building spree reflecting the new
affluence and the plentiful supply of labor.

Asians also flourished during this Little Climatic Optimum, build-
ing large temples, setting up trading systems, creating great art
and literature, and inventing new agricultural implements. In North
America, the Anasazi Indians built their pueblos while other native
Americans farmed what is now western Wisconsin and eastern
Minnesota.

With the onslaught of colder weather at the end of the 13th century,
the good times of the High Middle Ages came to an abrupt halt.
Except during a few periods of clement weather, famine, plague,
and warfare were to torment mankind for the next few centuries.

As noted, not all regions or all peoples benefited from a shift to
a warmer climate in the past and the same is true of the present
and future. Some locales may become too dry or too wet; others
may become too warm. Certain areas may be subject to high pressure
systems that block storms and rains. Others may experience the
reverse. On the whole, though, mankind has benefited and will
continue to benefit from an upward tick in the thermometer. Warmer
weather means longer growing seasons, more rainfall overall, and
fewer and less violent storms.

History teaches us that warmer is better, colder is worse. The
optimal way to deal with potential climate change is not to strive
to prevent it (a useless activity in any case, as we shall see) but to
promote growth and prosperity so that people will have the
resources to deal with any shift, whether toward a warmer or a
colder climate.

3. The Health Effects of Global Warming

Introduction

Many researchers, environmentalists, and politicians forecast that rising world temperatures in the next century will have devastating effects on human health (NRC 1991; Mitchell 1991; Cline 1992; Gore 1992; IPCC 1992). Referring to the world as a whole, Working Group II of the Intergovernmental Panel on Climate Change (1995b, SPM-10) asserted: "Climate change is likely to have wide-ranging and mostly adverse impacts on human health, with significant loss of life." The authors of the IPCC report feared that increases in heat waves would cause a rise in deaths from cardio-respiratory complications. They also foresaw a rise in vector-borne diseases, such as malaria and dengue and yellow fevers. The report did acknowledge briefly that, in colder regions, there would be fewer cold-related deaths.

Most of the causes of premature death have nothing to do with climate. Worldwide the leading causes are chronic diseases—accounting for 24 million deaths in 1996—such as maladies of the circulatory system, cancers, mental disorders, chronic respiratory conditions, and musculoskeletal disorders, none of which has anything to do with climate but everything to do with aging (*World Health Report* 1997, vol. 2, no. 1.). Another 17 million, most of them in poor countries, succumbed in the same year to disorders caused by infections or parasites, such as diarrhea, tuberculosis, measles, and malaria. Many of those diseases are unrelated to climate; most have to do with poverty.

Diarrheal diseases, such as cholera and dysentery, killed 2.5 million of the 52 million people who died worldwide in 1996. Through the provision of fresh water and proper sanitation, those diseases are easily preventable. Although a warmer climate might make the environment more hospitable for such afflictions as cholera, dysentery, and typhoid in areas without good sanitation or clean water, chlorination and filtration could halt their spread.

Both the scientific community and the medical establishment assert that the frightful forecasts of an upsurge in disease and early mortality stemming from climate change are unfounded, exaggerated, or misleading and do not require action to reduce greenhouse gas emissions. *Science* magazine reported that "predictions that global warming will spark epidemics have little basis, say infectious-disease specialists, who argue that public health measures will inevitably outweigh effects of climate" (Taubes 1997). It added: "Many of the researchers behind the dire predictions concede that the scenarios are speculative." The American Council on Science and Health has recommended that spending to reduce greenhouse gas emissions will make societies poorer and that any additional outlays should go instead to such public health measures in developing countries as improving drinking water and sanitation, vector control, medical infrastructures, and systems of emergency response to extreme weather events (Shindell and Raso 1997).

This chapter examines the effect of climate and, in particular, temperatures on mortality in the United States. Anecdotal evidence suggests that warmer temperatures may actually promote health. Folklore alleges that physicians sometimes recommend that patients escape to a more clement climate, never to a colder one.

The few studies that have examined in depth the relation between warming and human health or mortality have focused either on increases in the number of days of very hot weather, which can increase mortality, or on the spread of infectious diseases by such vectors as mosquitoes, flies, and snails (Smith and Tirpak 1989; Kalkstein 1991; Stone 1995). Nevertheless, several major studies of the implications of global warming for the United States have neglected or claimed a lack of data on its effects on health or human welfare (NRC 1978; Nordhaus 1991; Cline 1992).

Other studies of the influence of climate change on human health have examined a rather narrow set of potential medical problems. The underlying research has generally referred to Lyme disease, malaria, dengue and yellow fevers, and encephalitis, none of which is a major health problem in the United States. The IPCC (1995b, p. SPM-10) has emphasized that the "geographical zone of potential malaria transmission in response to world temperature increases at the upper part of the IPCC-projected range (5° to 9°F by 2100) would increase from approximately 45 percent of the world population to approximately 60 percent by the latter half of the next century."

Concern about tropical and insect-spread diseases seems over-blown. Inhabitants of Singapore, which lies almost on the equator, and of Hong Kong and Hawaii, which are also in the tropics, enjoy life spans as long as or longer than those of people living in Western Europe, Japan, and North America. Both Singapore and Hong Kong are free of malaria, but that mosquito-spread disease ravages nearby regions. Modern sanitation in advanced countries prevents the spread of many scourges found in hot climates. Such low-technology and relatively cheap devices as window screens can slow the spread of insect vectors. The World Health Organization (1990, 21) notes:

> until recent times, endemic malaria was widespread in Europe and parts of North America and . . . yellow fever occasionally caused epidemics in Portugal, Spain and the USA. Stringent control measures . . . and certain changes in life-style following economic progress, have led to the eradication of malaria and yellow fever in these areas.

Under the stimulus of a warmer climate, insect-spread diseases might or might not increase. Many of the hosts or the insects themselves flourish within a relatively small temperature or climatic range. Plague, for example, spreads when the temperature is between 66° and 79°F with relatively high humidity but decreases during periods of high rainfall (White and Hertz-Picciotto 1995, 7-7-3). Higher temperatures and more rainfall are conducive to an increase in encephalitis. Malaria-bearing mosquitoes flourish under humid conditions with temperatures above 61° and below 95°F. Relative humidity below 25 percent causes either death or dormancy.

Parasitic diseases, such as AIDS, Lyme disease, yellow fever, malaria, and cholera, can usually be controlled through technology, good sanitary practices, and education of the public. Even without warming, it is certainly possible that dengue fever or malaria could invade North America. Unfortunately, some of the government's well-meaning environmental policies may make the vector more likely. The preservation of wetlands, although useful in conserving species diversity, also provides prime breeding grounds for mosquitoes that can carry the diseases. If the United States does in the future suffer from such insect-borne scourges, the infestation may have less to do with global warming than with the preservation of swampy areas.

Torrid Summers

Recent summers have sizzled. Newspapers have reported the tragic deaths of the poor and the aged on days when the mercury reached torrid levels. Prophets of doom forecast that rising temperatures in the next century portend a future of calamitous mortality. Scenes of men, women, and children collapsing on hot streets haunt our imaginations.

Happily the evidence refutes that dire scenario. First, however, let us review the documentation supporting the supposition that human mortality will rise with rising temperatures. Death rates during periods of very hot weather have jumped in certain cities, but above-normal mortality has not been recorded during all hot spells or in all cities. Moreover, research concerned with "killer" heat waves has generally ignored or downplayed the reduction in fatalities that warmer winter months would bring.

In a 1991 paper, Laurence Kalkstein, one of the most respected and careful scholars examining the health effects of climate change, finds that deaths are related to the length of the hot spell. He suggests that it takes an extended heat wave to raise the death rate. In a later work, he reports that heat spells early in the summer or quick rises in temperature trigger deaths; in other words, unseasonal or rapid warming produces mortality (Kalkstein 1992). But if rapid warming causes deaths, we should find that most of the mortality during heat spells occurs on the first day or so and that fatalities then taper off, rather than increase with the length of the warm spell. As indicated, Kalkstein finds the opposite: deaths go up after a long spell of hot weather.

Kalkstein also finds that a particular weather pattern—characterized by high temperatures, strong southeast winds, moderate humidity, and relatively clear skies with little cloud cover—is correlated with increased mortality in St. Louis. For other cities either no weather pattern was related to mortality or the patterns that correlated with extra deaths differed. Even in St. Louis, many of the days that exhibited the suspect weather showed no unusual number of fatalities. Moreover, very hot days, those with temperatures over 100°F, failed to show death rates higher than the rates on those days when the thermometer made it only to 95°F. In fact, the number of recorded deaths in St. Louis during that particular weather pattern varied considerably more than during other periods, which reduces our confidence in the results.

Researchers analyzing hot days and deaths have found no constant relationship; even when extremes in weather and mortality are correlated, the relationship is inconsistent. Cities with the highest average number of summer deaths are found in the Midwest or Northeast while those with the lowest number are in the South (Kalkstein and Davis 1989, 56). Typically analysts have failed to find any relationship between excess mortality and temperature in southern cities, which experience the most heat (Kalkstein 1992, 372). Other studies have found that people who move from a cold to a subtropical climate adjust within a very short period (Rotton 1983). Moreover, Kalkstein and others have reported without explanation that the "threshold" between temperatures that lead to excess deaths and those that have no effect varies significantly among the cities. In some, such as Los Angeles, San Francisco, Boston, and Pittsburgh, the threshold was below 85° while in Phoenix and Las Vegas, it exceeded 110°F.

Scholars have also reported contradictory and implausible results. According to several analyses, air pollution is not correlated with premature deaths (Kalkstein 1991). Some studies have found that during hot spells mortality goes up sharply in females; other researchers have measured increased deaths among men (Kalkstein 1992 using Applegate et al. 1981, Bridger et al. 1976, Ellis 1972). Blacks are apparently more susceptible in St. Louis; whites, in New York. The lack of agreement on the effects of weather and on premature deaths again raises suspicions about the robustness of the results.

Measurement error may also foul up daily figures. In 1995, for example, Chicago suffered through an extraordinarily hot July that the press characterized as a harbinger of global warming. The coroner reported a marked increase in deaths. What was very curious was that on Friday, Saturday, and Sunday, July 14, 15, and 16, the reported deaths were way below the normal of 78 per day—only 14 people were reported to have died on Saturday—but on the two following days, Monday and Tuesday, fatalities were well above normal. The previous record low body count for any day in the last 30 years had been 46! Given that on Friday, July 14, a record temperature of 106°F was measured at Midway Airport, those numbers are not only remarkable but suspicious. Could it have been that most people in the coroner's office took the hot weekend off and counted bodies on Monday and Tuesday?

Researchers have attributed the absence of heat-related deaths in southern cities to acclimatization and the prevalence of housing that shields residents from high temperatures. In the North, the housing of the elderly and the poor is usually old and dilapidated. Over the next hundred years, if not sooner, most of those buildings will be torn down and replaced. Should the climate warm, builders will move toward structures that protect the inhabitants from extreme heat, as housing in the South allegedly does now.

These findings may imply simply that out-of-the-ordinary high temperatures increase the mortality of those in a weakened state. Studies have found that those most likely to die during heat spells are elderly (Kalkstein and Davis 1989, 62; Kalkstein 1992). Little attention has focused on the question of whether excess deaths represented only premature mortality of a few days among the old or sick or whether the excess deaths shortened lives significantly. Studies examining excess deaths by months fail to find any positive correlation with high temperatures, indicating that any daily excess is offset by a reduction in fatalities over the next few days. In the South, where temperatures are routinely very high during the summer, even the elderly adjust. Consequently, if the climate becomes warmer, no excess deaths can be expected.

Fear of killer heat waves appears exaggerated. If temperatures rise slowly over the next century, possibly by the 2° to 6°F currently predicted, people will become acclimated while housing can and, in the normal cycle, will be replaced. After all, half the housing stock in the United States has been built during the last 25 years. Consequently, if warming takes place, people and housing will adapt; even if extended warm spells occur, mortality should not rise sharply. Moreover, the models and the evidence to date suggest that most of the warming will take place in the winter and at night. Consequently extreme heat events are unlikely to become much more common.

Heat-stress does increase mortality; but it typically affects only the old and infirm, whose lives may be shortened by a few days or perhaps a week. There is no evidence, however, that general mortality rises significantly. The numbers of heat-stress-related deaths are very small; in the United States they are exceeded by the number of deaths due to weather-related cold. During the latest 10-year

Figure 3-1
PROPORTION OF WEATHER-RELATED COLD DEATHS TO
HEAT-STRESS MORTALITY

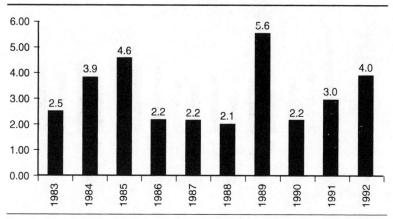

SOURCE: *Vital Statistics of the United States* (1983–1992).

period for which we have data (figure 3-1), which includes the very hot summer of 1988, the average number of weather-connected heat deaths was 132, compared with 385 for those who died from cold. Even during 1988, more than double the number of Americans died from the cold than passed on from the heat of summer. A somewhat warmer climate would clearly reduce more deaths in the winter than it would add in the summer.

Mosquito-Borne Diseases

A growing chorus has been chanting that global climate change will spread insect-borne diseases, such as malaria, dengue fever, and yellow fever, to temperate latitudes. In 1996, the health effects of global warming have been the subject of lengthy journal articles in the *Journal of the American Medical Association* (1996), and *Lancet* (1996), an international journal of medical science and practice. In September 1996, the Australian Medical Association sponsored a major conference on the subject. Professor Paul Epstein of the Harvard School of Public Health claimed that in the past few years mosquitoes carrying malaria and dengue fever had been found at higher altitudes in Africa, Asia, and Latin America. In North America, David Danzig (1995), in a Sierra Club publication, has

Figure 3-2
REPORTED CASES OF MALARIA IN THE UNITED STATES

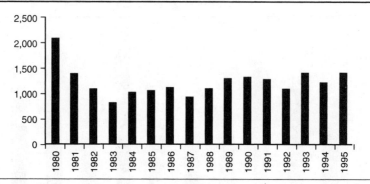

SOURCE: Centers for Disease Control and the *Statistical Abstract of the United States*, 1984–1996.

contended that only the tip of Florida is currently warm enough to support malaria-carrying mosquitoes but that global warming could make most of us vulnerable. He should check his history.

Before the Second World War, malaria was widespread in the United States. The Centers for Disease Control and the *Statistical Abstract of the United States* for the relevant years reported that over 120,000 cases were reported in 1934; as late as 1940, the number of new sufferers totaled 78,000. After the war, reported malaria cases in the United States plunged from 63,000 in 1945 to a little over 2,000 in 1950 to only 522 in 1955. By 1960, DDT had almost eliminated the disease; only 72 cases were recorded in the whole country. In 1969 and 1970, the CDC reported a resurgence to around 3,000 cases annually, brought in by service personnel returning from Vietnam. Subsequently, immigrants from tropical areas have spawned small upticks in new cases.

In the 1980s and 1990s, as Figure 3-2 shows, the number of reported cases has averaged around 1,200 to 1,300 annually. The CDC reports that since 1985 approximately 1,000 of those cases have been imported every year, with visitors and recent immigrants accounting for about half. The rest come from travelers arriving from tropical countries, service personnel returning from infested areas, and a handful of individuals, typically those living near international airports, bitten by a mosquito that hitched a ride from a poor country.

More stringent efforts to keep out the unwanted "immigrants" may be called for if the problem worsens.

Yellow and dengue fevers were both common in the United States from the 17th century onward. Epidemics of yellow fever ravaged New Yorkers and killed tens of thousands of people. In one year, 1878, of 100,000 cases reported along the East Coast, 20,000 people died. Between 1827 and 1946, eight major pandemics of dengue fever overran the United States. In 1922, the disease spread from Texas, with half a million cases, through Louisiana, Georgia, and Florida. Savannah suffered with 30,000 cases, of which nearly 10,000 had hemorrhagic symptoms, a very serious form of the disease. In contrast, in 1996 the CDC listed 86 imported cases of dengue and dengue hemorrhagic fever and eight local transmissions, all in Texas. There were *no* reported cases of yellow fever.

As a public health issue, those diseases, which did plague the United States in the reputedly colder 19th and early 20th centuries, have been largely exterminated. There is no evidence that a resurgence is imminent. Certainly the climate is not keeping the spread of the diseases in check. If it was warm enough in the cold 19th century for the mosquitoes to thrive, it is warm enough now!

Is there any basis at all for these scare-mongering prophecies? Is malaria rising worldwide? Not according to the World Health Organization. As Figure 3-3 shows, from 1983 to the latest year for which data exist, 1992, the number of cases of malaria reported in Africa, the most heavily infested section of the world, has fallen sharply, especially in the most recent years. For the rest of the world, reports are somewhat less encouraging. Malaria continues to be a problem, but there has been no increase in cases reported even though the world's population has climbed. The good news is that the rate of malaria per 100,000 people has fallen for the whole world.

What brought an end to the scourges? The introduction of DDT clearly played a major role. From the end of World War II until it was banned in 1972, the pesticide worked wonders to eliminate harmful insects, espcially mosquitoes. But it was not just insecticides that did the trick. Simple steps, such as screens on windows, the elimination of standing water, and the movement to the suburbs, which reduced population density and thus the risk of transmission, have played a critical role in eliminating mosquito-borne diseases.

In 1995, however, a dengue pandemic afflicted the Caribbean, Central America, and Mexico, generating around 74,000 cases. Over

Figure 3-3
REPORTED MALARIA CASES IN AFRICA AND IN THE REST OF THE WORLD

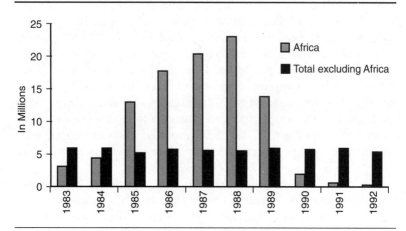

SOURCE: World Health Organization, Malaria Control Program, Geneva, Switzerland.

4,000 Mexicans living in the Tamaulipas state, which borders Texas, came down with the disease. Yet Americans living a short distance away remained unaffected. The contrast between the twin cities of Reynosa, Mexico, which suffered 2,361 cases, and Hidalgo, Texas, just across the border, is striking. Including the border towns, Texas reported only 8 nonimported cases for the whole state.

The only reasonable explanation for the difference between the spread of dengue in Tamaulipas and its absence in Texas is living standards. Where people enjoy good sanitation and public education, have the knowledge and willingness to manage standing water around households, implement programs to control mosquitoes, and employ screens and air-conditioning, mosquito-borne diseases cannot spread. If the climate does warm, those factors will remain. In short, Americans need not fear an epidemic of tropical diseases.

Cholera

A recent manifestation of fear-mongering about the health effects of global warming is a curious article in *Science*, taken from a modified text of Rita Colwell's presidential address to the American

Association for the Advancement of Science's 1996 annual meeting (Colwell 1996). This address presents a studious analysis of cholera and its recent resurgence in the Americas. What is most singular is not what is in Dr. Colwell's report but what she does not mention. Despite the title of the address, "Global Climate and Infectious Disease: The Cholera Paradigm," climate change is scarcely broached, and the one reference to it comes in connection with malaria, not cholera. Certainly Colwell makes no effort to tie global warming to the spread of cholera. Moreover, in a section strangely entitled "Global Climate, Global Change, and Human Health," the word "climate" does not appear; nor do the words "warmer," "temperature," or "global"! Also puzzling for such a careful exposition is the absence of any reference to the role that the Environmental Protection Agency may have played in creating the conditions leading to the explosion of cholera in Peru in 1991. But more on that later.

First, a few dry facts about cholera, an infectious disease caused by *Vibrio cholerae*, a bacterium that can bring on diarrhea, vomiting, and leg cramps. Without treatment, a person can rapidly lose body fluids, become dehydrated, and go into shock. Death can come quickly. Treatment is simple, the replacement of the fluids and salts with an oral rehydration solution of sugar and salts mixed with water. Fewer than 1 percent of those who contract cholera and are treated die.

Cholera cannot be caught from others but comes from ingesting food or water that contains the bacterium. Eating tainted shellfish, raw or undercooked fish, raw vegetables, or unpeeled fruits can lead to infection. Drinking unpurified water can be dangerous as well. The bacterium thrives in brackish warm water but can survive, in a dormant state, both colder water and changes in salinity. *V. cholerae* is also associated with zooplankton, shellfish, and fish. It often colonizes copepods, minute marine crustaceans. Ocean currents and tidal movements can sweep the bacterium, riding on copepods, along coasts and up estuaries where *V. cholerae* can remain dormant until conditions are ripe for it to multiply.

In 1817, the British first identified this dreaded disease in Calcutta, whence it spread throughout India, Nepal, and Afghanistan. Ships carried it into Asia, Arabia, and the ports of Africa. It reached Moscow, its first port of call in Europe, in 1830, creating panic as locals fled the city. From there it traveled to Poland, Germany, and

England. In the decade after it first appeared in Europe, it killed tens of thousands in Paris, London, and Stockholm. It reached North America in 1832, appearing first in New York and Philadelphia, then spreading along the coast to New Orleans. In that same year, the disease killed over 2,200 people in Quebec. Apparently cholera is not a tropical disease; it can kill and sicken in any climate, although in high latitudes it may do so only in the summer.

Before the most recent outbreak, the world suffered six cholera pandemics. By the end of the 19th century, however, Europe and North America were free of the disease. The solution was simple: filtration and chlorination of the water supply. Filtering alone not only reduces the spread of cholera but cuts typhoid significantly. Combining filtration with chlorination eliminates waterborne diseases. A warmer climate, if it were to occur, would not reduce the effectiveness of water purification measures.

In January 1991, after many disease-free decades, cholera began sickening villagers in Chancay, Peru, a port less than 40 miles north of Lima. It then spread rapidly up and down the coast. From that outbreak to the end of 1995, Latin America reported over 1 million cases—many went unreported—and 11,000 deaths. The illness traveled from Peru to Ecuador, Colombia, then Brazil. Eight months after appearing in Peru, it reached Bolivia. By the end of 1992, virtually all of South and Central America, from Mexico to Argentina, had confirmed cases. In the early 1990s, cholera also entered the United States; however, with the exception of a few cases brought on from eating raw, tainted shellfish, virtually all cases were contracted abroad. Seventy-five cases, nearly half the total 160 reported to the CDC between 1992 and 1994, originated on a single flight from Lima in 1992!

What went wrong to bring an end to Latin America's 100 years of freedom from cholera? Rita Colwell theorizes that an El Niño* led to a plankton bloom that multiplied the hosts of *V. cholerae*. But El Niños have been occurring with some regularity for many years

---

*A warming of the ocean surface off the western coast of South America that occurs every 4 to 12 years when upwelling of cold, nutrient-rich water does not occur. It causes plankton and fish to die and affects weather over much of the world.

Figure 3-4
TEMPERATURE VARIATION FROM NORMAL OFF THE
PERUVIAN COAST

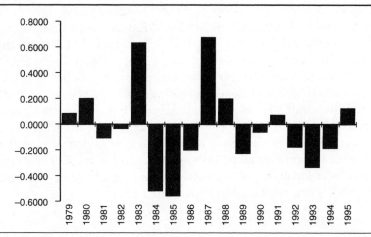

SOURCE: "EPA in the Time of Cholera," *World Climate Report 2*, no. 10 (February 3, 1997): 2.

without producing a cholera epidemic. As Figure 3-4 shows, the coast of Peru in 1991 was not even particularly warm compared with a number of other years. Even if El Niño were in part the culprit, the basic cause lies elsewhere. On the basis of EPA studies showing that chlorine might create a slight cancer risk, authorities in Peru decided not to chlorinate their country's drinking water (Anderson 1991). Perhaps they also thought they would save money. Chlorination, however, is the single most effective preventive of cholera and other waterborne diseases. After the fiasco in Peru, the EPA determined in 1992 that there was no demonstrable link between chlorinated drinking water and cancer. It was too late; the harm had been done. Peru's misplaced environmentalism led to more than 300,000 victims in that country alone.

Cholera is a disease of poverty, crowding, and unsanitary conditions. A warmer climate will not carry the disease to affluent countries; but in the Third World, economic growth can bring freedom from it and many other diseases. We should not impose costs on ourselves or others that would reduce the resources needed to bring clean water and good sanitation to Latin America, Africa, and Asia.

Overall Health Effects

A number of researchers have found a negative relationship between temperature and mortality and/or a correlation between season and death rates (Momiyama and Katayama 1967, 1972; Bull and Morton 1978). G. M. Bull and Joan Morton, British researchers, for example, reported that deaths from myocardial infarction, strokes, and pneumonia fell with higher temperatures in England and Wales. In New York, however, they fell only until the temperature reached 68°F and then rose with the heat. Momiyama (1963) found that deaths followed a seasonal path but that, in the United States, this pattern had been reduced in the period from the 1920s to the 1960s. Even though a regimen of increased deaths in the winter is apparent for all portions of the United States, England and Wales, and Japan, many subsequent researchers have emphasized summer deaths attributed to high temperatures.

Seasonal Effects

If climate change were to manifest itself as warmer winters without much of an increase in temperature during the hot months, which some climate models predict, the change in weather could be especially beneficial to human health (Gates et al. 1992). The IPCC reports that, over this century, the weather in much of the world has been consistent with such a pattern: winter and night temperatures have risen while summer temperatures have fallen (Folland et al. 1992).

A warmer globe would likely result in the polar jet stream's retreating toward higher latitudes; in the Northern Hemisphere, the climate belt would move north (Lamb 1972, 117, 118; Giles 1990). Thus an average annual 6.7°F increase in temperature for New York City, for example, would give it the climate of Atlanta. New York City's summertime temperatures, however, would not go up commensurably: the average high temperature in Atlanta during June, July, and August is only 4°F warmer than New York City's and the latter city has on record a higher summer temperature than does the capital of Georgia. Summer temperatures generally differ less than winter temperatures on roughly the same longitude and differ less than average temperatures.

According to the National Climatic Data Center, a sample of 45 metropolitan areas in the United States shows that for each increase of a degree in the average annual temperature, July's average temperatures go up by only 0.5°F while January's average temperatures climb by 1.5°F. Since warming will likely exert the maximum effect during the coldest periods but have much less effect during the hottest months, the climate change should reduce deaths even more than any summer increase might boost them.

Deaths in the United States and most other advanced countries in the middle latitudes are higher in the winter than in the summer. Except for accidents, suicides, and homicides, which are slightly higher in the summer, death rates from virtually all other major causes rise in winter months; overall mortality from 1985 to 1990 was 16 percent greater when it was cold than during the warm season (Moore 1998). These data suggest that, rather than increasing mortality, warmer weather should reduce it; but that possibility is rarely discussed.

Earlier studies have also reported the relationship between season and death rates. Professor F. P. Ellis of the Yale University School of Medicine noted that deaths in the United States between 1952 and 1967 were 13 percent higher daily in the winter than in the summer (Ellis 1972, 15, table II). The difference is smaller than experienced during 1985–90, a period that included some of the hottest summers on record. Ellis's study covered a time during which recorded average temperatures in the United States were somewhat lower than during the 1985–90 period. If hot weather were detrimental to life, the differential between summer and winter death rates during the latter period should have been smaller, not larger.

The increase in average temperatures during this century has apparently been accompanied by a decline in hot weather deaths relative to winter mortality. Before the early or middle part of the century, deaths during the summer months were much higher relative to winter than is currently the case (Momiyama 1977). Perhaps the decline in physical labor, which is afflicted with a much higher rate of fatal accidents than office work, helps to explain the change. One Japanese scholar, Masako Momiyama, however, reports that for most advanced countries, such as the United States, Japan, United Kingdom, France, and Germany, mortality is now concentrated in the winter.

A number of studies, as indicated above, have examined death rates on a daily basis (Bull and Morton 1978; Kalkstein and Davis 1989; Kalkstein 1991). This allows the authors to compare extreme temperatures with mortality. Although the research has shown that it is typically the elderly or the very sick who are affected by temperature extremes, the analyses ignore the degree to which this shortens life. Is it a few days or a few weeks? That cities in the South fail to show any relationship between deaths and high temperatures suggests that the correlation in the North may stem from deaths of the most vulnerable when the weather turns warm. One way to parse out whether climate extremes shorten lives by only a few days, or whether they lead to more serious reductions in the life span, is to consider longer periods.

Monthly data on deaths and temperatures, for example, show that deaths peak in the cold period. My research finds that monthly figures on various measures of warmth are correlated with monthly deaths in Washington, D.C. (Moore 1998). The results support the proposition that climate influences mortality.

Although deaths peak in the winter, factors other than cold, such as less sunlight, could induce the higher mortality. The peaking itself does not prove that warming would lengthen lives; it could be that the length of the day affects mortality. The day's length is closely correlated with temperature, of course, but, unlike the amount of sunlight, which remains constant each year, temperature fluctuates from year to year. My research, however, indicates that the length of the day is correlated with the death rate but is less statistically significant than temperature (Moore 1998). Moreover, if measures of temperature are combined with the length of the day, the amount of sunlight loses its statistical significance. Temperature remains the most important variable.

The District of Columbia study probably underestimates the relationship of deaths to temperature because some elderly from the capital winter in warm climates and die there. Nevertheless, the results imply that a 4.5°F warming—the "best estimate" of the IPCC under a CO_2 doubling—would cut deaths for the country as a whole by about 37,000 annually (IPCC 1992, 16).

Climatic Effects

Comparing death rates in various parts of the United States can provide evidence about how humans are affected by different climates. Within the continental United States, people live in locales that are subtropical, such as Miami, and cities that are subject to brutally cold weather, such as Minneapolis. The contrast between American cities makes the climate variables stand out. Within the United States, most people residing in big cities eat a more or less similar diet, live roughly the same way, and employ the same currency. Differences among the populations of various parts of the United States are confined largely to the age distribution, ethnic concentrations, income, and, of course, weather.

In a recent study, I expanded the research from a single city to the effect of climate on death rates around the country. Clearly many factors affect mortality. Within any population the proportion that is old influences death rates. Since African-Americans have lower life expectancies than whites, the proportion that is black affects mortality rates. Income and education also are related closely to life expectancy. As is well known, smoking shortens lives. Severe air pollution has pushed up mortality, at least for short periods.

As expected, age had the largest effect on death rates. The proportion of African-Americans is also highly significant in explaining death rates across counties. The higher the median income, the lower the death rate. Holding demographic and economic variables constant, I found that death rates are lower in warm climates. Various measures of climate demonstrate that warmer is healthier or at least extends life expectancies—once the age structure is held constant, there is a well established direct relationship between death rates and life expectancies. The analysis implies that if the United States were enjoying temperatures 4.5°F warmer than today, 41,000 fewer people would die each year (Moore 1998). That saving in lives is close to the number I estimated based on monthly Washington, D.C., data for the period 1987 through 1989.

In summary, the monthly figures for the city of Washington, between 1987 and 1989, indicate that a 4.5°F warmer climate would cut deaths nationwide by about 37,000; the analysis of climate in counties around the United States points toward a saving in lives of about 41,000. Those data sets produce roughly the same conclusion: a warmer climate would reduce mortality by about the magnitude of highway deaths, although the latter deaths are more costly in that they involve a much higher proportion of young men and women.

Morbidity

Presumably, if a warmer climate reduced deaths, it would also cut disease. In the early 1970s, the U.S. Department of Transportation sponsored a series of conferences on climate change that examined, among other things, the effect of climate on preferences of workers for various climates and on health care expenditures. At that time, the government and most observers were concerned about possible cooling of the globe. The department organized the meetings because it planned to subsidize the development and construction of a large fleet of supersonic aircraft that environmentalists contended would affect the world's climate.

The third gathering, held in February 1974, examined the implications of climate change for the economy and people's well-being and included a study of the costs to human health from cooling, especially any increased expenses for doctors' services, visits to hospitals, and additional medication (Anderson 1974). For that meeting, the Department of Transportation asked the researchers to consider a cooling of 2° Celsius (3.6° Fahrenheit) and a warming of 0.5°C (0.9°F). Robert Anderson Jr., the economist who calculated health care outlays, made no estimate of the costs or savings should the climate warm; but his numbers show that for every 5 percent reduction in the annual number of heating degree days, a measure of winter's chill, health care costs would fall by $0.6 billion (1971 dollars).[†] In a paper summarizing the various studies on economic costs and the benefits of climate change, Ralph D'Arge (1974), the principal economist involved in the DOT project, indicated that a 10 percent shift in heating degree days would be equivalent to a 1°C change in temperature. Thus the gain in reduced health costs from a warming of 4.5°F would be on the order of $3.0 billion in 1971 dollars or $21.7 billion in 1994 dollars, adjusting for population growth and price changes (using the price index for medical care).

In a more recent study, I examined the relationship between the number of hospital beds per 100,000 and the number of physicians per 100,000 and the average annual temperature. Although the number of physicians is only weakly related to climate, the number of hospital beds is significantly inversely related. In other words, holding income, race, and age constant, the warmer the climate, the lower the number of hospital beds or doctors. Assuming that the numbers of hospital beds and physicians reflect correctly the health care needs

---

[†]Each degree that the average temperature for a day falls below 65° Fahrenheit produces one heating degree day. If the mean temperature on a particular day were 60°, for example, the number of degree days would be 5. If the high for a day were 60° and the low 40°, the average would be 50° and the number of degree days would be 15.

of their communities and are an index of health care costs, the numbers suggest that, had the climate been 4.5°F warmer, private expenditures on health care would have been lower by $19 billion to $22 billion in 1994. Those numbers are remarkably close to the updated figures reported by Professor Robert Anderson ($22 billion). Assuming that government health expenditures would be affected comparably, the total national savings in medical costs would be about $36 billion.

That figure understates the benefits of warming because it does not include the gains from a reduction in suffering or from a cut in working days lost through disease. A minimum estimate of those gains would include the wage-cost of people with jobs who, in the absence of warming, would not have been at work because of illness. The $36 billion also neglects the gain to those who, because of the better climate, remain healthy and are not in the paid workforce or would have come to work in spite of suffering from a cold or the flu. If we assume that a 4.5°F warmer temperature would reduce illness by the same amount it is estimated to reduce deaths (1.8 percent) and apply the average workers' compensation, the savings come to around three-quarters of a billion dollars (*Statistical Abstract of the United States 1994*, 404, table 631; 427, table 660). These numbers also do not include any lowering of government expenditures on health care. Conservatively, health care saving would amount to about $37 billion per year.

Conclusion

Although it is impossible to measure the gains exactly, a moderately warmer climate would be likely to benefit Americans in many ways, especially in health. At the same time, let me stress that the evidence presented here is for a *moderate* rise in temperatures. If warming were to continue well beyond 4.5°F, the costs would mount and at some point the health effects would undoubtedly turn negative.[‡] Contrary to many dire forecasts, however, the temperature increase predicted by the IPCC, which is now less than 4.5°F, under a doubling of greenhouse gases would yield health benefits for Americans.

[‡]Adding minimum temperature squared or average temperature squared to regressions produced coefficients that were not only negative but insignificantly different from zero.

In summary, a warmer climate should improve health and extend life, at least for Americans and probably for Europeans, the Japanese, and people living in high latitudes. High death rates in the tropics appear to be more a function of poverty than of climate. Thus global warming is likely to prove positive for human health.

4. Weather Benefits and Other Environmental Amenities

The debate on climate change has usually focused on health, rising sea levels, increases in violent weather, or damage to agriculture. People's preferences for climate and for other amenity benefits, such as biodiversity, have received less attention. Rarely has research explored man's predilection for less chilly weather. Pleasant weather as well as a world populated with a diversity of living creatures are considered desirable and meaningful amenities. Men and women appear to prefer a world populated with living things, at least, at a distance. Although not all species are favored—reptiles, insects, and bacteria, to name a few, are not always welcome—most people want to maintain a globe inhabited by a large variety of animals, plants, and fish. Climate activists warn of a world with shrinking numbers of species as a warmer earth destroys their habitat. This chapter explores the public's taste for weather and for other intangible values that might be affected by climate change.

Given the circumstantial evidence that people favor warm climates over cold, it is somewhat surprising that the effects of warming on human well-being have been essentially ignored. We do know that, upon retiring, many people flee to southern and warmer locales. According to a 1966 survey of Americans turning 50 in 1996, almost 40 percent planned to move when they retired and the most important criterion in selecting their destination (40 percent) was a "more favorable climate" (*USA Today*, May 13, 1996, B1). People retire to Florida, not Minnesota. Presumably retirees, at least, find that higher temperatures improve their welfare. As air-conditioning has mitigated the rigors of hot summers, the population of the United States has been moving south and west, toward regions that suffer less extreme cold weather. Most Americans and Canadians taking vacations in the winter head to Florida, the Caribbean, Mexico, Hawaii, or southern California. Exceptions crowd the ski slopes, but they are a minority.

To my knowledge only one study—summarized in the U.S. Department of Transportation research described in the previous chapter—has examined human preferences for various climates, an important measure of how weather affects human welfare (Hoch and Drake 1974). Many studies examining the quality of life in various urban areas, however, have found that warmer climates are correlated with a willingness to accept lower wages (Hoch and Drake 1974; Hoch 1977; Cropper and Arriaga-Salinas 1980; Cropper 1981; Roback 1982, 1988; Gyourko and Tracy 1991). As a gauge of preferences, that research and this chapter both use workers' willingness to pay for a better climate as measured by the differential in wages among cities.

Human Well-Being

In *The Wealth of Nations*, Adam Smith pointed out that workers must be paid more to work in an unpleasant place or to do nasty jobs (Smith 1937, 100–18). A casual examination of the job market illustrates the truth of that proposition. Oil companies must pay their workers premiums to cope with the climate on the North Slope of Alaska. Even in central and southern Alaska, labor commands higher wages than it does in the lower 48 states. The differentials reflect the desirability of jobs in one area over another. Those who have the least distaste for cold and darkness, for example, can be lured for the smallest premium to Prudhoe Bay, Alaska, to work in the oil fields. The differential reflects the marginal valuation of the unpleasantness of work in that harsh environment for those with the least aversion to the conditions.

Theory of Amenity Values

There is a large and growing economic literature on such amenity values, that is, on characteristics that people value (Hoch 1977; Rosen 1979; Cropper and Arriaga-Salinas 1980; Graves 1980; Cropper 1981; Roback 1982, 1988; Blomquist et al. 1988; Graves and Waldman 1991; Gyourko and Tracy 1991). Locational advantage can be reflected in the willingness of workers to accept lower wages or in the bidding up by business and home buyers of land values (Roback 1982). If land values are raised enough, wages could even be forced higher to maintain real incomes. It is likely, however, that if workers willingly work for less in a region that they find attractive, the amount in wages that they are willing to forgo *understates* the benefits of the location. Some benefits have probably been capitalized into land values and are reflected in higher housing costs. Living costs are raised, thus reducing the amount of wages that workers will sacrifice to live where it is pleasant.

The relationship of wages to locational values becomes more complicated if the desirable qualities of the area affect the costs of the firm either positively or negatively. If businesses face higher costs because of the attractiveness of the area, wages must be lower for the firm to locate in a high-cost region. Companies planning to market nationwide that might prefer to build a plant in Hawaii, for example, would face much higher shipping costs both for supplies and to market their products in the continental United States. In effect, workers must accept a lower wage to induce employers to locate in a city or area that imposes higher costs on them.

Alternatively, if the amenity lowers the costs for the firm, more and more businesses will move to the area, boosting land costs. Eventually land costs will rise enough to discourage both employers and employees from locating in that favorable environment. The San Francisco area is a good example: its desirability for business and for many people has boosted land costs enough to force up wages. Generally we cannot predict whether good weather and other amenities that attract business and boost land costs will also raise or lower wages. Will the desirability of a location be so great that workers would be willing to accept lower pay even though they must pay more for housing?

Studies of the Effect on Land Values

A number of economists have examined the relationship of locational factors, such as the climate, to land values. Professor Jennifer Roback of George Mason University, for example, found that no climate factors had any significant relationship to land values (Roback 1982, 1272, table 3). Glenn Blomquist from the University of Kentucky and his economist colleagues from Kentucky and Michigan State University reported that precipitation, humidity, heating degree days, and cooling degree days were negatively related to housing expenditures—a proxy for land values—while wind speed, sunshine, and being close to the coast were positively related (Blomquist et al. 1988). Even though statistically significant, both cooling and heating degree days had very small effects on housing expenditures. Taking into account the effects of heating and cooling degree days on both wages and housing costs, the full implicit price of those variables was trivial. Two other economists, Joseph Gyourko of the Wharton School and Joseph Tracy of Yale University, reported that their measure of housing expenditures fell with greater precipitation, a greater number of cooling degree days, more heating degree days, and higher wind speed (Gyourko and Tracy 1991). On the other side, they also found that the higher the relative humidity and the closer to the coast, the higher the housing costs.

In sum, existing studies have reported mixed correlations between housing costs and weather-related values. Gyourko and Tracy (1991, 784) conclude their analysis of amenities by finding that "for many city traits, the full price largely reflects capitalization in the labor rather than in the land market." The rest of this chapter, therefore, will assume that climate amenities have no effect on production costs; as a result, any measured wage reduction underestimates the benefits from warming.

Studies of the Effect on Wages

Economic studies have examined the relationship of amenities to wage rates. One of the first was the DOT's third conference on global climate change, referred to above, which used differences in occupational wages among urban areas to estimate the value of climate to workers. One of the tables, presented by Ralph D'Arge in his overview of the economic research, drew on the work of Irving Hoch, professor of economics at the University of Texas, to supply estimates of the costs and benefits of a 0.5°C warming (D'Arge 1974, 569). Hoch's research implies that a rise in temperature would bestow on workers an implicit gain of $1.6 billion in 1971 dollars (Hoch and Drake 1974). In other words, adjusting for 1995's level of wages and salaries and assuming that the temperature/wage relationship is linear, workers in 1995 would have been willing to accept about $47 billion less in wages for working in a 4.5°F warmer climate.

Although Professor Roback discovered no significant relationship between climate and land values, she did find that heating degree days, total snowfall, and the number of cloudy days were positively correlated with wages, all of which suggests that those are disamenities (Roback 1982, 1270). As expected, the number of clear days was negatively correlated with wages. She also found that the colder the winter (heating degree days), the higher the wages (Roback 1988). In summary, she was able to say that workers like warm weather without much snowfall in the winter and with few cloudy days. They must be paid more to put up with cold winters.

Economist M. L. Cropper of the World Bank reported an inverse correlation between July temperatures and wages for a variety of occupational groups (Cropper 1981). Not all the occupations exhibited statistically significant temperature relationships; but, with the exception of sales workers, all wages were inversely correlated with temperature, implying that workers preferred warm weather. An earlier paper, written with Professor A. S. Arriaga-Salinas, reported that the coefficient for July temperature was also negatively related to wages (Cropper and Arriaga-Salinas 1980). Their research supports the proposition that people like warm climates.

Expanding the scope of the research, Gyourko and Tracy reported that heating degree days were positively correlated with weekly wages (Gyourko and Tracy 1991, 782, table 1). In other words, the colder the weather, the higher the wages. Both precipitation and wind speed, however, were significantly negatively correlated with wages, a somewhat puzzling result. The results imply that people favor warm but windy, wet climates. Professor Glenn Blomquist and his colleagues, on the other hand, found that both heating degree days and cooling degree days were negatively correlated with their hourly wage variable, implying that workers like both cold and hot weather (Blomquist et al. 1988, 95, table 1).

All the studies show that hotter summers are related to lower wages. On the other hand, all the studies, except that of Blomquist et al., found that the lower the temperatures, the higher the wage. He reported that the warmer the January readings, the higher the wage, a peculiar finding. Except for the work by Blomquist and his colleagues, therefore, all these studies find that workers prefer hot summers and warm winters.

Empirical Results

This author, following Hóch's work, related wage figures to climate in various cities (Moore 1998). Data for 1987 from the Bureau of Labor Statistics on wage rates for secretaries, auto mechanics, and computer programmers (49 cities), word processors (43 cities), and tool and die makers (36 cities) were correlated with average annual temperatures and other climatic variables.

The relationship between hourly earnings and measures of annual temperature, the size of the population, and seasonal change produced the best results. Seasonal change was measured by the difference in the average high temperatures in July and the average low reading in January. A number of independent variables that might plausibly affect the desirability of various metropolitan regions were tried, including the crime rate, days that the city was in violation of the EPA's ozone standard, heating degree days, cooling degree days, the proportion of the population in the central city that was black, annual precipitation, plus a dummy variable for the South. None of these proved significant.

These statistical comparisons indicated that workers prefer warm climates to cool; they also like climates with substantial seasonal changes in temperature. This might explain the anomalous results of Blomquist and his colleagues mentioned above. The results suggested that the gains from a warmer world might range from as low as $30 billion to a high of $100 billion. Hoch's work, reported above, implies a gain of about $50 billion, a figure well within the predicted range.

Should warming lead to a bigger boost in winter temperatures and a smaller rise in summer, as suggested previously, the gain from higher temperatures would be offset in part by a decline in seasonal variation, leading to a smaller dollar benefit. If the entire rise in temperatures came in the nighttime (9°F), thus boosting winter lows with no rise in the day, seasonal variation would fall by 9°F and average temperatures would rise by 4.5°. In that case, since seasonal change would be reduced significantly without raising maximum temperatures, workers would be worse off by around $10 billion. On the other hand, if the rise in temperatures reflected the current relationship of average temperature to average winter temperature (increases of 1.5° for every degree the annual mean goes up) and to average summer temperature (rises only 0.5°), as mentioned in Chapter 3, the gain would be only $10 billion annually.

Analysis of Results

In all likelihood, these estimates of the value workers attribute to climate conditions underestimate substantially the tradeoff workers would make for warmer temperatures. If a warmer climate reduces costs to business by lowering transportation expenses, for example, land values will have to be bid up to achieve equilibrium. People attempting to locate in preferred areas will compete to find housing, making it more expensive for them as well as for companies. The higher rents mean that workers must be paid more to compensate. Thus the estimate of the value of a less frigid climate may be much too low. In addition, well-paid individuals prefer to live in pleasant climates, typically raising average incomes even of those who are less skilled.

Although it is impossible to measure the gains exactly, a moderately warmer climate would be likely to benefit Americans in many ways, especially in health and in satisfying people's preferences for more warm weather. Most people would enjoy higher temperatures, and the evidence supports the proposition that humans would live longer and avoid some sickness. Less cold weather would mean less snow shoveling, fewer days of driving on icy roads, lower heating bills, and reduced outlays for clothing. Technically, the beneficial results described apply strictly only to the United States, but it seems likely that advanced industrial countries in the middle or higher latitudes would benefit as well.

Valuations of Environmental Amenities

On the downside of climate change is the prospect of the loss of various species that are unable to adapt. Although paleontologists estimate that roughly 99 percent of all species that have ever existed have become extinct, most people feel it is a tragedy to lose additional unique animals and plants. The general public and scientists both value species for aesthetic, moral, and practical reasons; in medical research, for example, various animals and plants can provide valuable hormones, chemicals, or genes.

Some environmentalists have claimed that it is a tragedy to lose a single species. Edward O. Wilson, one of the world's most distinguished biologists, has contended that it is vital to protect all species (Wilson 1992). Although no one knows how many different species exist, many environmentalists claim that more species are going extinct than ever before. Given the evidence of mass extinctions in earlier epochs, that claim seems exaggerated.

Nevertheless, the issue has evoked concern. On May 21, 1997, 21 scientists sent a letter to President Clinton warning him that climate change would threaten biodiversity. They asserted that "climate change, in combination with existing anthropogenic habitat disruption and loss, could lead to steep declines in worldwide biodiversity." According to the group, the speed of climate change would strongly affect the ability of species to adapt.

Current evidence suggests the opposite. Several scientists have recently reported an increase from 1981 to 1991 in plant growth in the northern high latitudes (Myneni et al. 1997). More vigorous plant development, while possibly choking out a few species, provides a more plentiful habitat for animals. Similar reports have originated in Australia where researchers have found that warmer weather, more rainfall, and perhaps greater CO_2 have led to bumper crops (Nicholls 1997). In this connection one should note that the IPCC has postponed and lowered its predicted warming of 4.5°F by 2040 to 3.6° by 2100 A.D., indicating that climate change will be considerably more gradual than believed previously. The evidence of greater growth in fauna, together with the lengthening of the period of any warming, suggests that fears of extinction of major species are overblown.

Moreover, biodiversity appears to be greatest in the tropics. Warm wet areas are more congenial toward species proliferation than are the temperate zones. Climate change is most likely to increase that portion of the globe that is moist and hot, thus increasing the potential habitat for many species. Plants and animals that have adapted to temperate or cold climates can move toward the poles. While cold climates are not devoid of animals and plants, the more frigid the climate, the more desert-like is the region, with only a small number of individual species. Antarctica is virtually free of plants and only a very few animals can withstand the rigors of that climate. A warmer, wetter world, therefore, is more likely to promote biodiversity than to destroy it.

African lakes, for example, teem with fish not found in other locales. Lake Malawi, a large lake (11,000 square miles) in East Central Africa, is home to more than 500 different species of fish, most of which are unique to that lake (Myers 1977). In comparison, the North American Great Lakes, an area nearly nine times the size of that African inland sea, contain only 173 different types of fish, with fewer than 10 endemic to those water bodies. Norman Myers (1977, 133), a Senior Fellow with the World Wildlife Fund, makes the point that "virtually every major group of vertebrates and many other large categories of animal have originated in spacious zones with warm, equable climates, notably the Old World tropics and especially their forests." He goes on to assert that "the rate of evolutionary diversification . . . has been greatest in the tropics." When he tries to assert the value to humans of this diversity, however, he falls back on the commercial value of plant-derived pharmaceuticals, a subject discussed below.

Climate change would, by definition, affect the pattern of temperature and rainfall to which animals and plants would be exposed. Although many species would adapt, especially as the change would take place over a considerable time period, not all would survive. In the pre-industrial world, animals and some plants adversely affected by a warmer world migrated northward to maintain a suitable environment. Environmentalists, however, now claim that humans have taken over so much of the globe that other animals might find it difficult to move northward. Moreover, those species that adjusted to a mountain ecology could move only a limited amount higher before reaching the summit. In both cases, a few species might not be able to survive.

In a higher CO_2 world, most plants would probably not be at risk. Although the temperature may well rise, an environment richer in carbon dioxide is likely to stimulate plant growth. Moreover, higher CO_2 levels induce a more efficient use of water in plants and make them more drought resistant. In addition, most models suggest that, worldwide, rainfall should increase. It would be perverse to assume that additional precipitation would fall only over the oceans. Nevertheless, there are some species of plants represented only by small numbers in very localized regions; some of these could become extinct.

If the earth warms slowly, as expected, almost all mammals could migrate to a climate that they found suitable. Ocean fish need not fear climate change; at worst they might have to swim farther north. Were local temperatures to rise to the point at which some species had difficulty reproducing and surviving, humans could and would transport and transplant many of them to more favorable climates. Certainly for cultivated plants and for domesticated animals, global warming should have little effect. It is true, nonetheless, that wild animals and many plants would have to adjust without human help and that unfortunately some of them might be threatened.

The Value of Biodiversity

Thomas E. Lovejoy, a noted environmentalist, asserts that (Reaka-Kudla et al., 1977, 8) "biodiversity matters to human beings in a variety of ways." He goes on to stress that many items that humans consume stem originally from animal and plant life. A variety of plants and animals facilitate biotechnological advances that can provide better crops or other useful products. Lovejoy maintains that "discoveries for the advancement of medicine and understanding of the life sciences constitute one of the most powerful ways in which biodiversity can contribute to human society" (Reaka-Kudla et al. 1977, 9).

In the same volume, Ruth Patrick, who holds the Francis Boyer Chair of Limnology at the Academy of Natural Science of Philadelphia, makes the case that a large number of species help promote the well-being and existence of other animals, plants, and insects (Reake-Kudla et al. 1977, ch. 3). Patrick seems to be saying that biodiversity is important because it is necessary for biodiversity. Actually she is making a more subtle and important point: virtually all species rely on other species to maintain themselves and their habitat. This includes humans. For example, we depend on plants to convert carbon dioxide, which we breathe out, to oxygen, which we breathe in. Plants and animals provide us with food, clothing, shelter, and an abundant amount of goods. Those species in turn depend on others to flourish.

Nevertheless, the loss of a class of living beings does not typically threaten other species. Most animals and plants can derive their nutrients or receive the other benefits provided by a particular species from more than a single source. If it were true that the extinction of a single species would produce a cascade of losses, then the massive extinctions of the past should have wiped out all life. Evolution forces various life forms to adjust to change. A few may not make the adaptation but others will mutate to meet the new conditions. Although a particular chain of DNA may be eliminated through the loss of a species, other animals or plants adapting to the same environment often produce similar genetic solutions with like proteins. It is almost impossible to imagine a single species that, if eliminated, would threaten us humans. Perhaps if the *E. coli* that are necessary for digestion became extinct, we could no longer exist. But those bacteria live in a symbiotic relationship with man and, as long as humans survive, so will they. Thus any animal that hosts a symbiotic species need not fear the loss of its partner. As long as the host remains, so will parasites and symbiotic species.

Measuring the value of biodiversity objectively is probably impossible. Certainly people value plants and animals and would prefer that most, if not all, survive. Most men and women would be happy to see the cockroach, the mosquito, and the fly disappear. The extinction of poison ivy and poison oak would raise few regrets. Unfortunately, they are not the plants and animals that are the most vulnerable.

Economists have sometimes proposed surveying the public to estimate how much people would be willing to pay to preserve some amenity, such as a particular class of animals. Such "contingency valuation" surveys are unlikely to elicit correct estimates of the importance of the item being asked about, since those being asked do not actually have to pay anything. Moreover, when asked the value of an amenity, the respondent is unlikely to want to appear heartless and unfeeling and so will volunteer some amount. Typically the surveys focus on some attractive animal, rather than a rat, insect, or repellent species. The IPCC reports on one survey that inquired how much the public would pay to preserve a particular "endangered species." The animals asked about included the bald eagle, the grizzly bear, the bighorn sheep, the whooping crane, the blue whale, the bottlenose dolphin, the California sea otter, the northern elephant seal, and the humpback whale (IPCC 1995c, 200). The values elicited ranged from $1.20 per year per person to $64 for those shown a video of threatened humpback whales. All the animals asked about have charm and sex appeal. Given the bias in this type of research, the figures have no validity. Even the IPCC authors say that one cannot simply sum the numbers to get an overall figure for the worth of biodiversity.

Some advocates of protecting species, such as the Union of Concerned Scientists, have argued that the animals' genetic pool could in the future prove of great benefit to humankind (UCS 1997). Within that huge pool of DNA may lie cures for cancer, heart disease, or more exotic ills. Genes code for—that is, provide the instructions for manufacturing—chemical compounds, which may provide the basis for pharmaceutical products. Pharmaceutical companies have already spent significant sums investigating naturally occurring chemicals and hormones that might provide real health benefits with the aim of finding compounds that can be modified to enlarge the pharmacopeia. Drug companies have recognized that evolution over hundreds of millions of years has developed many natural substances of benefit to human life. Preserving that diversity is important, therefore, to humankind. According to that view, the value of such diversity is immeasurable.

In keeping with this line of thinking, the United States has signed the Biodiversity Convention, prepared for the United Nations Rio meeting in 1992. That agreement commits the signatories to respect the sovereignty and property rights of local governments over any genetic resources or compounds discovered on their lands. Merck and Company has signed an agreement with Costa Rica to pay $1 million and substantial royalties for any product developed or discovered from indigenous plants or animals. Other companies and countries are negotiating similar agreements.

Being skeptical about the vital importance of maintaining every single species is tantamount to being against motherhood—at least before Paul Ehrlich convinced the world that babies were bad—so one is reluctant to question the importance of species diversity. Nevertheless, the usefulness of any one species, at least as a potential pharmaceutical, is probably low. Although the number of species on the globe is unknowable, it is certainly large: it has been estimated to be at least 10 million, of which scientists have identified about 1.4 million, about half of which are insects (Simpson et al. 1996, 176; UCS 1997). Among plants, there is considerable duplication in the production of chemical substances. Many creatures and plants have similar needs and consequently manufacture comparable compounds. As a result, identical drugs or comparable drugs can be produced from different species, either because evolution has led to the independent development of very similar chemicals in various species or because closely related plants or animals produce comparable compounds. The number of other plants or animals that produce like chemicals affects the worth of any one species. If many varieties of plants produce the same compound, the importance of any one kind is minimal. On the other hand, if very few code for therapeutic chemicals, the cost of discovery becomes excessive and the prediscovery desirability of any single species, negligible.

Moreover, if a species is found over a wide range, its value in any one area will be limited (Simpson et al. 1996). If all animals or plants in that species produce the chemical, additional individual members are redundant. Consequently, the worth of preserving any particular region that harbors the valued plant or creature may be very small.

A new substance's contribution toward more effective medical treatment determines its ultimate benefit, but it has to compete with existing drugs. Alternative drugs may be equally effective in dealing with medical problems. Even if a plant variety is unique, it may still provide no additional benefits over substances already known. Thus chemicals isolated from new species must compete with like substances found in other species and with existing known drugs. Finally, synthetic drugs based on inorganic chemicals often can be just as effective.

As economists David Simpson, Roger Sedjo, and John Reid of Resources for the Future point out, the value of a marginal species may be small. The worth of any species in the wild must take into account the cost of finding a representative by trained taxonomists who must carefully record its location and appearance. A sample must be dried, ground, and prepared for analysis, not a simple task. Extracts must be tested to measure the active compounds. All of this is expensive and takes time. According to Simpson and his associates, more than 10 years are required from the time of the discovery of a potentially valuable species until a new pharmaceutical substance is ready for sale (Simpson et al. 1996, 168). In part as a result, over recent decades drug companies have developed annually only a handful of new therapeutic drugs; the FDA approves only about 30 new substances a year, of which perhaps 10 are derived from plants. Those costs imply that the importance of unknown species may be quite low.

The Resources for the Future group has made an effort to value the marginal species under assumptions that maximize its worth. They take as their basis that of all the different types of plants, 250,000 plant species might each produce a useful drug. Making some reasonable assumptions, they calculate that the value of the marginal type of plant is less than $10,000. In their work, they assume a probability of a successful find that *maximizes* the value of the marginal variety. A higher or lower probability of making a hit would cut its value. This follows because the more species with an appropriate substance, the less valuable any single one will be; but the fewer there are, the more false alarms, and the more searching required.

These economists translate their findings into an estimate of the value of protecting a marginal piece of land. That estimate depends on the species diversity of the area. For the richest territory with the greatest diversity (western Ecuador), they estimate that the benefit of the marginal hectare is only $8.00 per acre. Other less species-intense areas are worth less, with California Floristic province* reckoned at 20 cents. The authors assert that these are upper estimates of the value.

Although people do like the concept of a globe inhabited by many different types of animals and plants, the value of any one or even many is not large in benefits provided to mankind. The Greek chorus of doomsayers grossly overstates the value of biodiversity. Their exaggerated veneration of each and every species leads to mistaken policy and needless expense.

---

*A region roughly bounded by Oregon in the north, the Pacific in the west, the Sierra Nevada in the east, and the Gulf of California in the south. This area is recognized by botanists as a separate evolutionary center, which contains one-fourth of all the plant species found in the United States and Canada combined. Half, or 2,140 species, are found nowhere else in the world.

5. The Economic Costs (Benefits?) of a Warmer World

Casual analysis of the economic effects of climate change demonstrates that most modern industries are relatively immune to weather. Climate affects principally agriculture, forestry, and fishing, which together constitute less than 2 percent of U.S. gross domestic product (GDP). Manufacturing, most service industries, and nearly all extractive industries remain unaffected by climate shifts. Factories can be built in northern Sweden or Canada or in Texas, Central America, or Mexico. Higher temperatures will leave mining largely untouched; oil drilling in the northern seas and mining in the mountains might even benefit. Banking, insurance, medical services, retailing, education, and a variety of other services can prosper as well in warm climates (with air conditioning) as in cold (with central heating). A warmer climate will lower transportation costs: less snow and ice to torment truckers and automobile drivers; fewer winter storms to disrupt air travel—bad weather in the summer has fewer disruptive effects and passes quickly; a lower incidence of storms and less fog will make shipping less risky. Fuel consumption for heating will decline, while that for air conditioning will increase.

Inhabitants of the advanced industrial countries would scarcely notice a rise in worldwide temperatures. As modern societies have developed a larger industrial base and become more service oriented, they have grown less dependent on farming, thus boosting their immunity to variations in weather. A few services, such as tourism, may be susceptible to temperature or precipitation alterations: a warmer climate would be likely to shift the nature and location of pleasure trips. Ski resorts, for example, might face less reliably cold weather and shorter seasons. Warmer conditions might also mean that fewer northerners would feel the need to vacation in Florida or the Caribbean. On the other hand, new tourist opportunities might develop in Alaska, northern Canada, and other locales at higher latitudes or upper elevations.

In many parts of the world, warmer weather should mean longer growing seasons. Should the world warm, the hotter climate would enhance evaporation from the seas, leading most probably to more precipitation worldwide. Moreover, the enrichment of the atmosphere with CO_2 would fertilize plants and make for more vigorous growth. Agricultural economists studying the relationship of temperatures and CO_2 to crop yields have found not only that a warmer climate would push up yields in Canada, Australia, Japan, northern Russia, Finland, and Iceland but also that the added boost from enriched CO_2 fertilization would enhance output by 17 percent (Wittwer 1995, 1997).

Several scientists have recently reported that the increased concentration of CO_2 has produced an increase from 1981 to 1991 in plant growth in the northern high latitudes (Myneni et al. 1997). More vigorous plant development, while possibly choking out a few species, provides a more plentiful habitat for animals.

Rising sea levels would, of course, impose costs on low-lying regions, including a number of islands and delta areas. For the United States—assuming a three-foot rise in sea level, at the high end of predictions for the year 2100—economists have estimated the costs of building dikes and levees and the loss of land at $7 billion to $10.6 billion annually, or less than 0.2 percent of GDP (Cline 1992, 109). For some small island nations, of course, the problems could be much more severe and their hardships should be addressed.

Past Studies

Few studies have evaluated the costs and the benefits from warming on human activity. Most have found only small costs to the advanced nations; even the rest of the world would suffer little. At least one major research effort, the U.S. Department of Transportation (DOT) study, has concluded that a warmer world would confer benefits on Americans.

Department of Transportation Study

The last two chapters discussed the 1974 U.S. Department of Transportation's findings on how climate affected health care expenditures and preferences of workers for various cities. The third gathering, held in February 1974, examined the implications of climate change for the economy. The DOT study brought together scholars from around the world (Broderick and Hard 1974). They included researchers from the following institutions: American Geophysical Union, Boston College, Boston University, Brookhaven National Laboratory, Colorado State University, Cornell University, Florida State University, Harvard University; Illinois Institute of Technology Research Institute, Institute for Defense Analysis, Lawrence Livermore Laboratory, Los Alamos Scientific Laboratories, Massachusetts Institute of Technology, Mitre Corporation, National Academy of Sciences, National Resource Council of Canada, New York University, North Dakota State University, Ohio State University, Pennsylvania State University, Princeton University, RAND Corporation, Rice University; Sandia Laboratories, Scripps Institute of Oceanography, Stanford Research Institute, Stanford University, Temple University, University of Colorado, University of California at Los Angeles, University of California at Riverside and at Berkeley, University of Florida, University of Kentucky, University of Illinois, University of Maryland, University of Michigan, University of Missouri, University of Pittsburgh, University of Rhode Island; University of Texas at Dallas, University of Washington, University of Wyoming, Utah State University, Wayne State University, Yale University; and in addition several Canadian, French, Russian, Polish, Japanese, and other foreign universities and research institutes. Clearly a comprehensive body of researchers contributed to the project.

Table 5-1 summarizes the findings of the DOT research. The numbers have been brought up to 1990 levels to reflect inflation over the period. As may be seen, cooler weather would be costly for the United States, while a warmer climate would produce small but positive benefits.

The Environmental Protection Agency Study

In September of 1986, after Senate hearings on the problems of global climate change, the Senate Committee on Environment and Public Works wrote the Environmental Protection Agency (EPA) requesting two studies, the first to examine the "health and environmental effects of climate change. This study should include, but not be limited to, the potential impacts on agriculture, forests, wetlands, human health, rivers, lakes, and estuaries as well as other ecosystems

Table 5-1
ECONOMIC COSTS OF COOLING AND WARMING: DOT STUDY
BY RALPH D'ARGE
(billions of 1990 dollars)

Impact	−2°F	+0.9°F
Corn production	+	−
Cotton production	−9.0	+
Wheat production	−8.7	
Rice production	−3.0	
Forest production	−2.1	
Douglas fir production	−1.5	
Marine resources	−4.5	
Water resources	+	−
Health impacts	−12.4	
Wages	−19.1	8.0
Residential, commercial, and industrial fossil fuel demand	−0.9	0.5
Residential and commercial electricity demand	3.9	−1.8
Housing and clothing expenses	−2.6	1.3
Public expenditures	−0.1	0.1
Corn Belt investment costs	−0.3	
Total	−$51.5	$8.0

SOURCE: D'Arge 1974, 568, table 1.
NOTE: Gains and losses of less than a billion are simply indicated by + and −.

and societal impacts" (letter to Lee Thomas 1986). The second study was to examine policy options that could stabilize current levels of greenhouse gas emissions.

The resulting study of the effects of climate change is a curious work. There is no reference to the earlier work done by the Department of Transportation, although it had been published only 12 years earlier. Unlike the DOT Climatic Impact Assessment report, which, as the previous section indicated, was conducted by serious scholars from around the world, the EPA report was crafted almost entirely by EPA staffers or their consultants.

The few outside experts called on by the EPA came from only a handful of organizations, most of them not in the top rank of research institutions. Even though the agency drew on scholars from Oregon

State University, University of California at Santa Barbara and at Davis, San Francisco State University, and the University of Delaware, no participant was connected with such major research centers as Stanford, Harvard, MIT, University of California at Berkeley, University of Michigan, National Academy of Sciences, Yale, or Princeton. The EPA study included no economists and produced few figures on the costs of warming.

Interestingly the authors of the EPA study assert that "the cities with the highest average number of summer deaths are in the Midwest or Northeast, and those with the lowest number are in the South" (Smith and Tirpak 1989, 224-5). This adds to the evidence in Chapter 3 that people adapt to warm weather but not to cold. Although the authors do say warming would reduce mortality slightly, overall the EPA's chapter on health appears to have chosen selectively those medical problems aggravated by high temperatures and generally ignored the effect of warmer winters.

Even though the discussion in the chapters suggests dire consequences, the EPA report to Congress fails to give any estimates of the costs of global warming. The chapters dealing with the effects cover Forests, Agriculture, Sea Level Rise, Biological Diversity, Water Resources, Electricity Demand, Air Quality, Human Health, Urban Infrastructure and regional studies of California, the Great Lakes, Southeast, and the Great Plains. The Report's findings on forests are typical:

> Global warming could significantly affect the forests of the United States. Changes could be apparent in 30 to 80 years, depending upon the region, the quality of the site, and the rate of climate change. There may be northward shifts in species ranges, dieback along the southern reaches of species ranges, and changes in forest productivity (Smith and Tirpak 1989, 71).

The other chapters have summary conclusions similar to those on forests. All predictions are hedged with "could," "may," and offsets, such as CO_2 fertilization acknowledged but played down. The major exception is for Sea Level Rise, which projects, for a one-meter rise (about three feet) of the oceans, a capital cost of $73 billion to $111 billion to prevent erosion and inundation through bulkheads, levees, and pumping sand (Smith and Tirpak 1989, 123). For the more likely one-foot increase, the total capital cost would be between $24 billion

Table 5-2
WILLIAM NORDHAUS'S ESTIMATES OF THE IMPACT OF DOUBLING
OF CO_2 FOR VARIOUS SECTORS

Sectors	Billions of 1990 Dollars
Severely impacted sectors:	
Farms (warming and CO_2 fertilization)	−15.2 to +13.9
Forestry, fisheries, other	small + or −
Moderately impacted sectors:	
Construction	+
Water transport	?
Electricity demand	−2.4
Nonelectric heating	+1.7
Water and sanitary	− ?
Sea level rise damage:	
Loss of land	−2.2
Protection of sheltered areas	−1.3
Protection of open coasts	−4.1
Hotels, lodging, recreation	?
Total	−$8.9 billion

SOURCE: William Nordhaus 1991, 932, table 6.

and $37 billion. Spread over 50 years and at a 3 percent real interest rate, the annual cost would be slightly more than $1 billion per year.

Nordhaus Study

A few economists have made separate studies of the effect of climate change on the United States. William Nordhaus, professor of economics at Yale University, for example, has done some of the best work on this issue (Nordhaus 1991, 920-37). After a careful analysis of the effects of global warming on the United States, he found that the total loss for the United States from a doubling of CO_2 would be roughly 0.26 percent of national income (Nordhaus 1991, 932, table 6). In the 1990 economy, that would be about $14.4 billion. Table 5-2 gives Nordhaus's estimate with the dollars changed to 1990 levels, using the GNP deflator. The total in the table is smaller than the $14.4 billion because the individual items are not adjusted for the growth in the economy from 1981 to 1990.

Nordhaus claims that the figures underestimate the cost of warming because they fail to reflect nonmarketed goods and services, such as human health, biological diversity, amenity values of life and leisure, and environmental quality. As earlier chapters have indicated, health and amenity values would be benefited by warming, not harmed; and the dollar loss from reduced biodiversity would be very small.

Air pollution, particularly smog, might increase as a result of more hot weather; but the cost to the public, while unmeasurable, is probably small. Los Angeles, with the worst smog in the nation, still attracts millions of people. Although Nordhaus acknowledges that the National Research Council in 1978 found substantial amenity benefits from global warming (Nordhaus 1991, 932; NRC 1978), he arbitrarily quadruples his estimate of the costs of warming to 1 percent of world income to reflect the unmeasured sectors, even though he admits that one study found large *benefits* from warming for one of those areas. Nordhaus then writes, "My hunch is that the overall impact upon human activity is unlikely to be larger than 2 percent of total output." How he got from one-quarter of 1 percent of GDP to 2 percent, he fails to explain; it seems to be nothing more than an exercise at arriving at a more politically expedient figure. Inexplicably, given his modest cost estimates, Nordhaus sponsored and signed the "Economists' Statement on Climate Change," which urged the government to take action to slow the emission of greenhouse gas emissions. There was also an "Economists' Statement on Climate Change" sent to President Clinton in 1997.

Cline Study

William Cline of the Institute for International Economics has produced one of the most extensive treatments of the subject (Cline 1992). Even though he is a strong advocate of taking action now to slow greenhouse gas emissions, after examining a number of sectors he concludes that the results of warming would be small. To achieve a benefit/cost ratio greater than 1, that is, a measure where the benefits from abating CO_2 exceed the costs, he inflates the benefits from avoiding climate change to take into account unaccounted costs. Cline first estimates the benefit/cost ratio at 3:4, that is, for every $3 of benefits, there would be $4 of costs, and writes, "The benefits of damage avoidance do not quite cover costs" (Cline 1992,

8). He then goes on to apply arbitrary weights to boost the benefits, managing in this way to boost the benefit/cost ratio above 1. He has abatement costs peaking at 3.5 percent of GNP in 2040 and 2.5 percent for the rest of the century. To really justify and reinforce his advocacy of abatement, however, he extends his forecasts out 300 years to 2300, a time period of which we can have no knowledge (Cline 1992, 4).

To vindicate further his call for emission reductions, Cline tends to use higher than the usual estimate of 4.5°F warming in his text but then labels his table specifying the cost of warming as attributable to a rise of 4.5°F. He often resorts to the 300-year predictions of 18°F warming to achieve meaningful losses.

As stated, any forecast based on 300 years must be considered speculation. We can have no idea what the world will look like then and there is no way for us to know. Three hundred years ago, the chief means of transportation was by foot or, for the more affluent, by a horse-drawn carriage; wood was the main fuel; energy was produced with human effort or through animals; life expectancies were about 40 years; electricity was unknown; real democracy was unimagined. With change occurring ever more rapidly, what will the world look like 300 years hence?

Cline's discussion of farming stresses drought but never once mentions the forecasts that world rainfall would increase. In his section on the construction sector, however, he quotes predictions by the General Circulation Models of 8 to 15 percent increase in rainfall. According to his book, it would rain on residential and commercial building, thus limiting any benefits; but it would not rain on farms, thus leading to more devastating droughts! He says that there would be an increase in precipitation in winter in mid-latitudes and a year-round rainfall boost in the high latitudes and in the tropics (Cline 1992, 122). At an American Economic Association session in January 1995, dealing with a forthcoming IPCC report, he asserted that drought would make water pollution more of a problem. In fact, since rainfall would rise, the reverse is true.

In leisure activities, he stresses skiing losses without mentioning that most outdoor activities, such as camping, golf, tennis, canoeing, hiking, and bicycling, would benefit from warming. Those activities absorb the time of more people than does skiing, which is one of the least popular outdoor recreational activities. Most people in the mid-latitude countries take their holidays in the summer; if they take them in the winter, it is to go South in search of warmth and sunshine. Nevertheless, Cline emphasizes skiing and its loss, ignoring that skiing can move north and that, with added precipitation, skiing might improve—the major difficulty most resorts experience today is lack of snowfall, not temperatures that are too warm. Although I am a fervent skier, the data show that most consumers are not and that they prefer warm weather recreation. At worst, it would seem that climate warming would produce a transfer of benefits from skiing to other forms of recreational activities.

Cline also stresses the areas that would receive less rainfall as opposed to those that would receive more. He expatiates on the Sacramento basin—a semiarid region and far from typical—and emphasizes that there would be less summer runoff as a result of less snowfall in the mountains. He fails to take into account the increase in winter runoff, which is just as good for filling reservoirs.

In discussing possible damage to water supplies, Cline asserts that "summertime precipitation would be unlikely to rise in mid-latitudes" (Cline 1992, 126). Four pages earlier he had written that there would be an *increase* in winter precipitation in mid-latitudes. He argues that there would be less cloud cover, yet acknowledges that the models predict greater total rainfall. If there is more rainfall, there must be more clouds. Actually the computer models are unable to predict where and how much rainfall will result from climate change. Any speculation about too little or too much rainfall in the winter or the summer or over the mountains or in California's Central Valley is just that, speculation.

Table 5-3 shows his estimates for the cost of global warming plus my own. I have reworked his figures and added other data to present another view and, in my opinion, a more accurate portrayal of the costs and benefits of climate change. The following sections describe the process used to arrive at the estimates. Two sectors of the economy that Cline ignored have been added; they are enclosed in brackets. The table values the human lives saved, as reported in Chapter 3 above, at $1 million each. Where the gain or loss is smaller than half a million, + and − are indicated in the table. The calculations also use the most conservative valuation of people's preferences for a warm climate. Under that conservative scenario, Americans would gain from a warmer climate about $100 billion dollars per year!

Table 5-3
ANNUAL BENEFITS (+) OR DAMAGES (−) FROM
GLOBAL WARMING FOR THE UNITED STATES
(billions of 1990 dollars)

Activity	Cline	Moore
Agriculture	−17.5	+
Forest loss	−3.3	+
Species loss	−4.0	−1.0
Sea level rise		
Construction of dikes, levees	−1.2	−0.6
Wetland loss	−4.1	−1.1
Dryland loss	−1.7	−0.4
Energy for heating and cooling residential homes and businesses	−9.9	+12.2
Human amenity		+10.0
Human life	−5.8	+40.0
Human morbidity		+37.0
Migration	−0.5	+0.2
Hurricanes	−0.8	−0.8
Construction		+4.4
Leisure activities	−1.7	+1.0
Water supply	−7.0	+5.6
Urban infrastructure	−0.1	+0.2
Air pollution		
Tropospheric ozone	−3.5	−2.2
[Transportation]		+0.3
[Marine resources]		+
Total	−61.6	+104.8

SOURCE: Information from Cline 1992, 131, table 3.4, and the author's calculations.

In 1996, the IPCC issued a controversial analysis, *Climate Change 1995: Economic and Social Dimensions of Climate Change,* prepared by Working Group III, which identified the damages that would occur under global warming. Several researchers, including William Cline, wrote Chapter 6, "The Social Costs of Climate Change: Greenhouse Damage and the Benefits of Control." Although the chapter pretends to present a balanced picture, it always portrays the most alarming possibilities and plays down any mitigating arguments or evidence.

For example, the section dealing with agriculture discusses a number of studies that find losses and occasionally small benefits from warming. It starts the discussion with an analysis that forecasts a 5 to 40 percent fall in yields in developed countries and a 40 percent rise in food prices worldwide (IPCC 1995a, 190). Nowhere does it mention the work by Mendelsohn, Nordhaus, and Shaw (1994) in the *American Economic Review*, the official journal of the American Economic Association. That research, discussed here, found very small losses or small gains to American agriculture. Nor does the chapter mention any of the other studies that have reported benefits (White and Hertz-Picciotto 1995; Kane et al. 1991; Wittwer 1995). Instead the section relies heavily on Cline's own work, which is biased toward finding damage.

The Effects of Global Warming

As mentioned above, most sectors of modern economies are mainly impervious to climate and consequently to climate change. Agriculture, forestry, and transportation, however, are significantly influenced by climate. People and nations are also subject to rising sea levels, increases in violent weather, energy costs for heating and cooling, and changes in recreational activities. Each of these topics is discussed below.

Agriculture

Food output depends largely on agriculture, an industry that would be particularly sensitive to any climate change. Water availability, soil composition, technology, sunshine, and temperature all affect crop production. Warm climates have longer growing seasons and higher productivity. Wetter areas, holding other factors constant, are more productive than dry, unless the latter are irrigated. Climate change, if it takes place, is most likely to lead to a warmer climate, especially in higher latitudes where it will have a strong beneficial effect on the length of the growing season. Climatologists predict that a warmer world would enjoy more rainfall. Although models are unable to forecast where rainfall will increase, most places should experience at least a little more. The net result of warming and enhanced precipitation would be to boost farm output.

In addition, the concentration of CO_2 in the atmosphere is rising. Carbon dioxide is an essential ingredient for plant growth. It boosts both photosynthetic capacity and water-use efficiency. According

113

to peer-reviewed research, a doubling of carbon dioxide would on average boost growth by 52 percent (Wittwer 1997, 12). Moreover, the improved water-use capacity of plants means that less rainfall would be needed to grow crops, thereby economizing on irrigation and perhaps offsetting partially any local reduction in rainfall (Baker and Allen 1994). As a consequence, a boost in carbon dioxide would have a strong beneficial effect on food production.

Evidence exists that rising levels of CO_2 have already hiked plant growth worldwide. Tests at Mauna Loa in Hawaii have not only documented a rise in the level of carbon dioxide in the atmosphere, from 316 parts per million in 1959 to 360 ppm in 1996, but shown a marked seasonal pattern that has become more pronounced (Wittwer 1997, 10). The levels of CO_2 in the atmosphere begin to fall in the northern spring as the new growth of plants absorbs the gas and reach a low by early fall. As plant growth ceases and leaves fall in autumn, CO_2 levels rebound to a mid-winter high. The amplitude of this pattern has been increasing, at least since 1960, by about 0.5 percent annually (Wittwer 1997, 11). This would suggest that plant growth worldwide has been on the upswing.

Additional evidence that agriculture has benefited comes from Dr. Ranga B. Myneni, a biologist at Boston University, and his colleagues who have found that, since 1980, plant growth, during the summer months, has become more vigorous north of the 45th parallel (Myneni et al. 1997). Inasmuch as there has been no measurable warming over this period—some areas have warmed while others have not—the result must stem from increased CO_2 concentrations. They report that the growing season has lengthened by 12 days and that plant growth has become 10 percent more energetic. Similar reports have come from Australia, where researchers have discovered that warmer weather, more rainfall, and perhaps greater CO_2 have led to bumper crops (Nicholls 1997).

In 1994 two scientists, Paul Knapp and Peter Soulé, compared a site in central Oregon that had been extensively surveyed in 1960 with its flora 34 years later. The region was almost inaccessible; climate had remained constant; human activity, given its remoteness, was negligible. They reported that the site had become much greener, with large increases in trees, perennial grasses, and western juniper. After systematically excluding all other factors, they concluded that the rise in CO_2 had boosted growth (Knapp and Soulé 1996).

Many studies have examined the relationship between warming and agricultural output. In a cautious report, the U.S. Department of Agriculture reviewed the likely influence of global warming on crop production and world food prices. The study, which assumed that farmers fail to make any adjustment to mitigate the effects of warmer, wetter, or drier weather—such as substituting new varieties or alternative crops and increasing or decreasing irrigation—concludes:

> The overall effect on the world and domestic economies would be small as reduced production in some areas would be balanced by gains in others, according to an economic model of the effects of climate change on world agricultural markets. The mode ... estimates *a slight increase* in world output and a *decline in commodity prices* under moderate climate change conditions (Kane et al. 1991, emphasis added).

Economists Robert Mendelsohn, William Nordhaus, and Daigee Shaw researched the relationship between climate and land values in the United States (1994, 753–71). After holding land quality, the proximity to urban areas and the nearest coast, and income per capita constant, they found that climate explained over two-thirds of the value of croplands. They concluded that, for the lower 48 states, a rise in average temperature of about 5°F and an 8 percent increase in rainfall stemming from global warming would, depending on the model used, reduce the value of output between 4 and 6 percent or boost the value of output slightly. The result ignored the effect of increased CO_2 on farm output. It is consistent, however, with the Department of Agriculture's study that suggests the United States might see a slight fall in output while production in the rest of the world increased.

Dr. Sylvan Wittwer, a professor of horticulture at Michigan State University, has concluded that, although scientists know little about the effect of climate change on food production, the benefits of increased levels of CO_2 are unambiguous. The distinguished professor emphasizes that

> the effects of an enriched CO_2 atmosphere on crop productivity, in large measure, are positive, leaving little doubt as to the benefits for global food security. ... The rising level of atmospheric CO_2 is a universally free premium, gaining in magnitude with time on which we can all reckon for the

foreseeable future. Direct effects of increasing CO_2 on food production and the output of rangelands and forests may be more important than the effects on climate (Wittwer 1995, 236).

Other studies such as those appearing in *Economic Issues in Global Climate Change: Agriculture, Forestry, and Natural Resources* generally find small costs or benefits. Most of those papers, however, fail to take into account the effect of CO_2 on output; those that do find it increases yields considerably. On the basis of those studies, Table 5-3 lists neither a gain nor a loss for the U.S. farming sector, a conservative position. If the effect of carbon dioxide fertilization adds to output and reduces world food prices, as the Department of Agriculture study suggests, U.S. producers may lose; but American consumers, as well as those in the rest of the world, will gain. In any case, I assume that the sum of the gain for consumers and any loss for producers from lower prices would be positive but close to zero.

Forest Loss

Forestry is another sector subject to change as a result of an increase in CO_2 and world temperatures. Canadian agricultural economists, examining the effect of warming and a doubling of CO_2 on forestry production, concluded that increased carbon dioxide would boost productivity by 20 percent and that overall the harvest of timber in Canada would climb by about 7.5 percent (Van Kooten 1990, 704). Although their research applies strictly only to our northern neighbor, it seems reasonable to infer that timber output in the United States could be more than maintained at current levels. If the climate changes, forest managers can shift the types of trees to fit the new environment.

Brent Sohngen of Ohio State University and Robert Mendelsohn of the Yale School of Forestry and Environmental Studies have estimated that the U.S. timber market would benefit from climate change by less than 1 percent to more than 10 percent of the current value of American forests (Sohngen and Mendelsohn 1996). British researcher J. L. Innes, for the Forestry Commission in Surrey, United Kingdom, reports that over the last 100 years, forests have expanded "in areas as far apart as southern Patagonia and northern Finland. As growth . . . is primarily controlled by temperature, it seems likely that climatic change is involved" (Innes 1994, 239). The IPCC has projected that global forest area could increase as much as 9 percent (IPCC 1996).

The total value of all lumber and wood products produced in the United States in 1993 was only $35 billion. If we assume that warming might increase production by 1 percent, the total gain would be less than $1 billion. Actually since the United States imported around $9 billion in that year, a substantial portion of consumption, world prices would affect domestic costs. A worldwide increase in production of 1 percent would reduce prices so that the total dollar value of the increase in U.S. output would be even less than $350 million. To be conservative I have not projected a dollar gain from warming, but timber prices should decline and consumers would benefit.

Species Extinction

Cline's estimate of the economic loss from species extinction is really nothing more than a number pulled out of the air. He asserts that the public was willing to spend $160 million to preserve the spotted owl and therefore might be prepared to spend 25 times that amount or $4 billion to preserve other species. No justification is given for multiplying by 25. Why not 10 or 100?

Moreover, the general public has not spent $160 million to preserve the owl; the timber companies have had losses inflicted on them to save the redwood forests in which the owl lives. The $160 million reflects the estimated value of the timber that was not cut. People like big trees; but in general the public has paid relatively little because timber has been imported from Canada to make up for the shortfall. Timber prices did increase somewhat, however. To the extent that the program to preserve old forests has driven up timber prices, the burden on the public has been hidden. In no way can it be argued that the voters decided that they would spend $160 million to preserve the spotted bird.

Chapter 4 examined the benefits of biodiversity for pharmaceutical research and concluded that, for the production of new drugs, its value was close to zero. It is true, of course, that all of us fancy a world populated with many species of animals and plants. Nevertheless, it would be surprising if the public were willing to pay more than $1 billion annually to preserve an unknown number and unknown types of species. That estimate has no more basis than does Cline's.

117

The media exaggerate the numbers of species that are becoming extinct. Of the 1,354 species here and abroad that have been listed by the Interior Department since 1966, only 19 have been delisted. Seven did become extinct; eight were listed in error; only four recovered enough to allow delisting. Three of those are native to the western Pacific; the fourth is a plant that grows only in Utah. None of the recoveries appears to have had anything to do with the protections of the Endangered Species Act. The handful of species that did go out of existence represents only .5 percent of all those listed and a much, much smaller proportion of those species identified and monitored. In all, there have been few identified extinctions in recent years, despite the rhetoric about wholesale losses of species, and an informed public is unlikely to pay much to prevent the loss of such small numbers.

Sea Level Rise

The IPCC concludes that a 4.5°F warmer world would lift sea levels by one to three feet, with the central estimate being about one and a half feet by the year 2100 (IPCC 1995c, 188). Cline assumes that the ocean would rise by one meter, about three feet. On the basis of the IPCC's central estimate that the sea will rise only about one and a half feet in the next 100 years, construction costs for dikes and levees are cut in half to $600 million annually from his figure of $1.2 billion.

To calculate the value of the land that would be submerged, Cline assumes that rental values of land would be 10 percent of the value of the land, too high a percentage. Abstracting for risk there is no reason that rental values for land should be higher than the long-run real rate of interest, about 3 percent. Cline also minimizes the discount rate by assuming it to be only 1.5 percent. From these assumptions, he calculates that the annual loss from the land inundated by a rising sea would be $5.8 billion. Adjusting those estimates to reflect a smaller rise in the sea and employing a real rate of interest of 3 percent for both rents and discounting pares his estimates to $1.5 billion, less than one-quarter of his figure.

Heating and Cooling Expenses

Warming will reduce the costs of home and office heating while increasing the costs of air conditioning. Ignoring business costs for heating and cooling and consumer expenditures for oil and gas heating, Cline considers only the consumer's outlays for electric heating and cooling. By focusing on electricity costs, he biases upward potential expenditures under a warmer climate because air conditioning, which would be used more, requires electricity. Homeowners can heat their homes, a cost that would go down, not only with electricity but with gas, coal, oil, or even wood, the benefits of which he ignores.

The U.S. Department of Energy estimated the savings in energy costs for both a 1.8° and a 4.5°F warming. They calculated that even with added cooling expenses, the gain would be about $12.2 billion for the greater gain in temperature (Rosenthal et al. 1995). I have adopted their estimate as being the most authoritative.

Human Amenities

William Cline argues that human amenity would deteriorate because of hot summers, although he admits that less ice and snow in the winter would be positive. We need only ask the following: "Do people prefer the summer or the winter?" "Do humans enjoy warm weather or cold?" "What proportion of vacationers in the winter go south and what proportion go to ski resorts?" The answer is obvious: people call warm weather "clement" and enjoy warm, sunny days.

The previous chapter reported on measures of amenity values. Those results have been confirmed independently by an Environmental Protection Agency staffer who surveyed the literature. The agency bureaucrat reported that individuals prefer climate change and are willing to accept lower wages for such improvements (IPCC 1995c, 201, based on Leary 1994). They also like sunny, mild climates. Those are essentially my conclusions.

My research implies that, assuming minimum temperatures and maximum all rise equally and depending on the statistical model, the gain from a warmer climate could be as little as roughly $30 billion or as much as $100 billion. If we assume that global warming will increase winter and night temperatures most, however, then the gain may be only $10 billion. Although the statistical procedures used to make these estimates undoubtedly underpredict the gains, Table 5-3 lists only the smaller figure.

Migration

Over recent decades, Americans have been moving south. Many retirees have left their cold northern neighborhoods and their friends and relations to migrate to warmer venues. Between 1984–85 and 1993–94, on net, over 300,000 people each year left the Northeast. The Midwest lost on average some 30,000 souls while the South gained over 250,000 and the West, over 100,000 (*Statistical Abstract of the United States 1995, 1996–97*, table 32). In 1992, revenue of household goods carriers transporting furniture and personal belongings between cities reached $7.4 billion (*Statistical Abstract of the United States 1996–97*, table 1024). That figure is an underestimate of the cash costs of moving, as many families rent vans or trailers. Ninety percent of all migrants from the Midwest and the Northeast in 1993–94 relocated either to the South or to the West. The implication is that about $3.0 billion was spent on commercial movers carting people's personal effects to the South or West. If warming simply reduced the desire of Americans to move south by 10 percent, it might save nearly $300 million annually in the costs of changing residences.

Mortality

Chapter 3 estimates that a warmer climate would reduce deaths by about 40,000 annually. If the lives saved reflect a random sample of the U.S. population, their value would be somewhere between $2 million and $10 million per life saved. These figures come from several studies of how much people are willing to pay to reduce the risk of early mortality (Viscusi 1994; Lutter and Morrall 1994). It may be, however, that the increase in length of life comes from adding a few years at the end. Putting a value on those extra years is problematical.

We know that diseases of the respiratory system, which account for 10 percent of all deaths in the winter, are over 50 percent higher in the cold season than during the summer. Diseases of the circulatory system, which account for about half of all deaths during the winter, are nearly one-quarter higher during December through February. The latter killer takes primarily older people whereas diseases of the respiratory system can sicken all ages. Thus, to be conservative, the 40,000 lives saved will be valued at only $1 million each for a total gain of $40 billion.

Human Morbidity

Not only should warmer weather extend lives, it should also reduce illnesses. A conservative estimate of the gain reflects simply the wage cost to people with jobs who are not at work because of illness. This neglects the gain to those not in the paid workforce and those who come to work even though they have a cold or the flu. I assume that a 4.5°F warmer temperature would reduce illness by the same amount that it would reduce deaths (1.8 percent). Workers' compensation consequently would fall by the same percentage, producing savings of around three-quarters of a billion dollars (from *Statistical Abstract of the United States 1994*, 404, table 631; 427, table 660).

Chapter 3 presented estimates of the reduction in hospital costs and in medical expenditures generally from a warmer climate. The savings in national expenditures on health care would be roughly $36 billion in a warmer world. Savings on workers' compensation come to nearly $1 billion. On net, therefore, global climate change, if it were to occur, should provide health benefits, aside from reduced mortality, of about $37 billion.

The analysis made of the costs of global climate change for the Department of Transportation in the early 1970s calculated the costs to human health from cooling, especially the costs of visiting a doctor or hospital and outlays for medication (Anderson 1974). Projecting the gains from a warmer climate and adjusting for the rise in medical expenses and the increase in U.S. population suggests a gain of about $22 billion. For the purposes of Table 5-3, the estimate of $36 billion on doctor and hospital costs, plus the savings on workers' compensation, were included for a total of $37 billion.

Hurricanes

Hurricanes develop over warm tropical water that provides both the moisture and the energy to fuel the storms. A warmer climate would lead to a larger portion of the oceans being covered by waters warm enough to support hurricanes. Moreover, a hotter world would also mean that the tropical oceans would remain warm for more of the year, producing longer hurricane seasons. In part, this would be offset by the reduction in the temperature differences between high latitudes and equatorial regions. Since temperature differences between the poles and the equator drive winds, storms overall, especially winter gales, blizzards, and cyclones, should be reduced. Nevertheless, hurricanes may become more common, so Cline's figures have been accepted. A proper accounting, however, would offset at least partially increased losses from hurricanes with smaller damage costs from other storms.

Construction

The IPCC report on the costs of climate change repeats Cline's strange rainfall results. Although much of the chapter stresses drought, the section on construction mentions that additional rainfall will hamper building activities (IPCC 1995c). Rainfall also is projected to inhibit outdoor activity, and losses to ski areas are again stressed.

Climate change should have only a very small effect on the building industry. Warmer winters, if they develop, will make it possible for construction firms to work more of the year. The longer work year would reduce costs modestly because contractors would be able to employ workers on a steadier basis. Not having to cope with as much snow and ice also should shave building costs. The implication is that the price of housing and other buildings would decline slightly, leading to some expansion of output. Nevertheless, the construction industry probably would build few additional housing units or office complexes, as the small reduction in costs is unlikely to have a noticeable effect on the volume of construction. The net effect, although likely to be small, would be positive, so the savings have been projected to be 1 percent of building costs, or $4.4 billion.

Leisure Activities

Most outdoor activity, with the exception of skiing and snowmobiling, would be helped by a warmer climate. Of 17 outdoor activities listed in the *Statistical Abstract of the United States 1994*, downhill skiing is 14th and cross-country skiing is 17th in popularity (*Statistical Abstract 1994*, 258, table 406). Only soccer and backpacking boast fewer participants than Alpine skiing. Thus the great majority of people who enjoy outdoor activities would find a warmer climate in their interest. The Europeans have estimated that tourism would improve in the European Union by about $4 billion (IPCC 1995c).

Additional spending on equipment and on entrance fees would reflect the minimum value consumers place on the benefits they would reap from being able to enjoy their favorite leisure activity for more of the year. If the amount spent on camping material, hunting gear, and golf clubs and accessories grows by 10 percent with a longer warm weather outdoor season while spending on ski equipment falls by the same percentage, consumers would, on net, increase their outlays on sports equipment by nearly $1 billion. For a number of activities that would also benefit from a longer season, such as hiking, softball, baseball, and football, outlays for equipment are unknown. Thus the $1 billion underestimates the gain to outdoor enthusiasts. That sum, moreover, does not include the additional spending on items like golf fees or the loss in ski lift charges. Since golf fees appear to be higher on average than lift tickets, the net result should be an additional gain, reflected in higher spending on golf over the loss to skiers. Table 5-3 uses the $1 billion gain, which is no doubt a considerable underestimate of the benefit of a longer warm season to sports participants.

Water Supply

Cline cites the 1990 IPCC report as concluding that world rainfall would increase by 8 percent (Cline 1992, 122). He assumes, however, that U.S. rainfall would decline by 10 percent. He predicates this assumption on two studies of water supplies in California, an area that is hardly typical of the entire country. The chapter Cline helped put together in the IPCC Working Group III report assumes a 10 percent decline in precipitation in 18 major water districts despite the climate model forecasts of increased rainfall (IPCC 1995c, 193). Taking the IPCC estimate of rainfall and employing Cline's methodology, the gain from *increased* rainfall would be $5.6 billion.

Urban Infrastructure

In discussing his forecasts of the effects of global warming on "urban infrastructure," Cline states that climate change will bring both more frequent droughts and more frequent heavy rains. He predicts that such a change will require additional outlays for expanding reservoirs and improving storm drains. The evidence, however, fails to show any such change in the weather over the last hundred years (*World Climate Report*, February 3, 1997 and March 17, 1997). It does show a rise since 1895 in average rainfall, which correlates with improved crop yields, but no increase in heavy rains.

Global warming, if it occurs, is expected to raise temperatures in high latitudes while having little effect on equatorial regions. As pointed out previously, fewer and less violent storms should affect the United States, with the possible exception of hurricanes, which are related to sea surface heating. Perhaps, between now and the year 2100, some cities may have to expand storm drains, but over such a period, they would have to be upgraded anyway, so the added cost would be minimal. On the other hand, as already mentioned, global warming should increase precipitation. On average, cities would have a more reliable water system and would need to invest less in expanding reservoir capacity, resulting in a net saving. Some areas, of course, could face diminished rainfall, but the majority of the country should gain precipitation.

In addition, winter weather would be less harsh and last for a shorter period, so northern cities should benefit. That would mean less spent on removing snow, salting the streets, heating municipal buildings, and repairing potholes, which are related to freezing. If we consider only those states where the principal cities suffer from average January lows below freezing—a consideration that excludes California and Texas, among others—total outlays by states and local governments in 1992 amounted to approximately $46.7 billion. Assuming that those communities and states would save only .5 percent on streets in reduced plowing, fewer potholes, less ice and snow removal, and less need for police traffic control and accident cleanup, the gain would be more than $200 million.

Air Pollution

Using EPA estimates, Cline points out, correctly, that warmer weather will lead to more smog and ozone. The EPA has concluded that a 7° rise in temperatures would increase peak ozone by 10 percent and has pinned the cost of offsetting the increase at $3.5 billion (Cline 1992, 129). Taking the numbers at face value and assuming a 4.5°F temperature rise, rather than 7°, the costs to mitigate the additional air pollution fall to $2.2 billion.

Transportation

Additional sectors of the economy, which William Cline ignored, might well be influenced by global climate change. In particular, transportation could gain from more clement weather. Less ice and snow would improve driving conditions and reduce weather-related delays for airlines. According to U.S. Department of Transportation figures, airline passengers suffer from greater delays in winter months than in summer. A warmer climate should improve on-time performance.

Currently the fewest delays occur during the third quarter, with the second and fourth quarter being better than the first. I assume that warmer temperatures would improve on-time performance during the cold months to the level of the second quarter (around 84 percent in 1992) from the poor showing during the first quarter (76 percent) and from the less good showing in the fourth quarter (81 percent).* Multiplying the percentage increase in on-time flights during those two quarters by the number of domestic passengers on all airlines operating aircraft larger than 60 passengers during the periods indicates that nearly 1 million people would benefit. Valuing airline passengers' time at a conservative average value of $20 per hour and assuming that average delays would be reduced by 30 minutes, warming would improve the well-being of airline travelers by about $100 million annually.

Airlines themselves would also gain: they would have fewer problems with aircraft being unable to land and diverted to other airports, a costly procedure. Dealing with irate passengers, rerouting them, putting them on later flights, providing meal tickets, and paying their hotel bills are expensive. Although airlines make virtually all their profits in the second and third quarters, thanks to increased numbers of passengers, their costs are slightly higher in the first and fourth, a reflection of poorer weather. If airlines could achieve the same costs in the two cold quarters as they do during the spring and summer, they would reduce their costs by $300 million.

Highway traffic should also benefit from improved weather and less snow and ice. Truck accidents are somewhat more frequent in the winter than in the summer—in 1987, the winter months experienced 6 percent more accidents than did the summer—but this could be ascribed to shorter daylight hours. Private auto travel is considerably reduced in winter months over summer—about 15 percent—and would become more balanced under global warming; that is, more people would visit their friends and relatives during the winter rather than concentrating their travel during the warm months. The result might be less congestion in the summer and an optimal use of the highway network. Although there would be clear

---

*Airlines in 1992 reported that during the third quarter 84.9 percent of their flights were on time, that is, arrived within 15 minutes of schedule.

gains to surface transportation from a warmer climate, a lack of data precludes any estimate of the benefit.

Marine Resources

Another sector Cline ignored is fishing. The Department of Transportation conference estimated the costs of cooling on fishing, both commercial and recreational. Economist Frederick W. Bell of Florida State University carefully reviewed the literature on the major types of fish caught commercially. Overall he reported (Bell 1974) that the present value of the loss from a cooler and drier world was $93 billion in 1974 dollars, or $138 billion in 1996 dollars.[†] Bell reviewed the effect that temperature, precipitation, and wind velocity would have on groundfish, tuna, salmon, halibut, sardines, shrimp, lobsters, crabs, clams, scallops, oysters, and other food fish, shellfish, and crustaceans. In the case of a decline in sea temperature and a fall in precipitation, the sustainable catch for all of the groups, except halibut, would fall by 1991. The decline in fish caught would be between 0.01 percent for crabs and 1.7 percent for salmon. Some of the loss would come from reduced rainfall, which would cut freshwater runoff in coastal areas. If rainfall were assumed to increase, production of shrimp, crabs, scallops, and oysters would go up in spite of the lower temperatures. Extending the period out to 2025 produced much larger changes.

On the basis of Bell's work, it might be reasonable to conclude that a warmer, wetter world would boost fish yields. Since a number of species thrive within a relatively narrow temperature band, however, this assumption may be unwarranted. Nevertheless, fish can adapt by swimming to cooler or warmer water, so that effect should be small. Although there is some evidence that warmer sea temperatures can boost yields—during the largest El Niño on record, 1982–83, which produced warm surface waters in the Eastern Pacific, fish prices went down—I will assume no overall benefit from climate change.

Total

Even though many potential advantages have not been included, Table 5-3 shows that Americans would benefit from warming by

---

[†]Adjusted using the food stuff and feed stuff crude materials price index of the producers price index.

126

Table 5-4
ESTIMATES OF COSTS OF GLOBAL WARMING
EXPECTED LOSS OF GDP

Researcher	U.S.A.	World
Cline (4.5°) 1992	1.1%	n.e.
Nordhaus (5°) 1991	1.0%	n.e.
Frankhauser (4.5°) 1995	1.3%	1.4%
Titus (7°) 1992	2.5%	n.e.
Tol (4.5°) 1995	1.5%	1.9%
Moore (4.5°)	Gain of 1.0%	n.e.

SOURCE: IPCC 1995c, 184, and author's calculations.
NOTE: n.e means no estimate.

over $100 billion per year. It seems almost indisputable that Americans would be better off at the end of the next century if temperatures were 4.5°F hotter than today. For the United States, Europe, Japan, and other advanced countries, it is implausible to assume that climate change would have overall significant negative effects. Thomas Schelling, in his 1991 presidential address to the American Economic Association, reported that for "developed countries, the impact on economic output will be negligible and unlikely to be noticed" (Schelling 1992, 6). Most likely, people would be oblivious to any change; they would simply enjoy the reduction in ice, snow, and cold.

Transition costs, such as the building of dikes, the introduction of new crops, or the construction of irrigation facilities, may exist. In part, those costs are included in the estimates of Table 5-3. Despite those adjustment costs, a warmer climate would almost surely benefit most Americans.

Virtually all the other estimates of the damages from global warming to both the United States and the world have been very small. For developed countries, they have ranged generally from 1 percent to 2 percent of GDP (IPCC 1995c, 184), although Nordhaus's original estimate was for one-quarter of 1 percent of GDP (Nordhaus 1991, 932). It is generally agreed that poor countries will typically fare worse than the advanced market economies. Table 5-4 presents some of those estimates as given by the IPCC in terms of the expected loss of GDP.

Some may be willing to grant that rich industrial countries in temperate climates might benefit, yet argue that the poor Third World areas will suffer. The IPCC Working Group III report asserts: ". . . climate change seems likely to impose greater risks and damage on poorer regions" (IPCC 1995c, 84). Chapter 3 of that report on "Equity and Social Considerations" argues strongly that poor countries are much more vulnerable, hence rich nations should bear the burden. Not only has the West produced most of the greenhouse gases to date—the rapidly growing Third World will soon exceed the output of the OECD countries—but the rich nations can afford to pay the cost of slowing or stopping global climate change and to contribute to any measures necessary to adapt to change. Climate policy has become foreign aid.

Poor countries dependent on agriculture are more sensitive to changes in climate. But the growth of CO_2 should actually help. Many of those nations are in tropical areas and will be largely unaffected because the climate will not change appreciably near the equator. Other subtropical regions should receive more rainfall and may benefit, although farmers may need to learn to grow new crops. Some low-lying countries—Bangladesh, for example—may suffer from more frequent sea flooding as water levels rise. Such places, including low-lying islands, may be the only major losers from warming. Rather than spend resources on a futile effort to slow warming, it might be more humane to help them either to accelerate their growth so they become less dependent on the weather, or to build dikes for protection from rising seas, as the Netherlands has done. Foreign aid should not be confused with environmental policy.

6. Slowing Greenhouse Gas Emissions: Politics and Costs

The previous chapters have shown that global warming would, in all probability, produce gains for most Americans. Somewhat higher temperatures would improve health, cut death rates, facilitate transportation, reduce heating bills, and help satisfy people's taste for warm weather. The major costs would come from higher sea levels and an increase in smog, which rises when temperatures climb. In most cases, those undesirable side effects could be mitigated at reasonable cost. From an American point of view, spending anything to reduce the emissions of greenhouse gases is unwarranted.

Nevertheless, the momentum to act has grown. Not everyone will agree that warming would be largely beneficial. Certainly parts of the world and even parts of the United States would be harmed from climate changes. To stop global warming totally, assuming the computer models are correct, is unrealistic. The IPCC has asserted that stabilizing atmospheric concentrations at no more than twice-current levels would require cutting emissions "substantially below 1990 levels" (IPCC 1995e). The cost of the latter step would be horrendous and so far few argue that we should go that far.

Nonetheless our leading newspapers and much political, environmental, and world leadership, to say nothing of the endless commentary on the network news programs, urge that America adopt measures to reduce greenhouse gases. Over 2,000 economists signed a statement calling for the government to take steps. Even the president and CEO of Chrysler Corporation, in a letter to the editor, wrote that "if in fact we are in a period of global warming, and if man is contributing to it, and if there's something we can do to slow it down, then we should act, and it may be prudent to assume the worst until we know better" (Eaton 1997).

Hysteria rather than rationality has taken over our discourse. A steady drumbeat of propaganda is stampeding the country into an unwise, expensive course.

Proponents of acting now to slow or even to prevent climate change start by suggesting that the United States, Western Europe, and perhaps the world adopt a "no-regrets" policy. The definition of such a policy varies with the author or authors. If it means policies sensible in themselves, few impartial observers would be opposed. The federal government, for example, sells water at heavily subsidized rates to California farmers who grow rice, a crop that generates massive amounts of methane, a major greenhouse gas. Eliminating the water subsidies would be economically efficient, even if policymakers were indifferent to possible climate change. Other sound policies might include inducing energy-producing nations, such as Venezuela, to refrain from providing their populace with extraordinarily cheap gasoline or urging former communist countries to allow oil, gas, and coal prices to rise to market levels. Increasing the use of nuclear energy would also be beneficial, both for the economy and, if people are concerned, for reducing greenhouse gas emissions.

Typically, however, no-regrets policies imply regulations designed to induce consumers and businesses to conserve fuel. Many advocates claim that the cost of those policies is negative, that is, they would bring economic gains in addition to any benefit from reduced greenhouse gas emissions. Such assertions are questionable. If consumers or businesses could save money by taking these steps, why do they not do it? Firms rarely pass up an opportunity to save energy and cut their costs. Individuals might be unaware of possible savings in the short run, but advertising and the media could and would inform people of potential gains. At best, government action could hasten the installation of energy-saving devices. Whether the resulting benefits from conservation would outweigh the drawbacks is doubtful. Champions of instituting those measures often overlook the convenience to consumers and industry of current practices, the cost of making the changes, and the potential unintended consequences. People usually are much more knowledgeable about their own concerns than some official in Washington or an environmental advocate preaching from a tax-exempt think tank.

Fuel economy standards are often suggested as a "cheap" or even "no-cost" way to save energy. The United States has experimented with such standards for autos and they are not cheap. Nor do they save much gasoline. In 1996, General Motors was forced to boost the price of its lowest-cost model by $200 to meet the latest exhaust standards (*San Jose Mercury News* July 25, 1996). To comply with earlier requirements, automobile manufacturers have installed expensive fuel-saving technology and made cars lighter, smaller, and consequently more dangerous than they need be, increasing highway fatalities (Crandall and Graham 1989; Moore 1991). Moreover, since driving the light, small car is cheaper—it travels farther on a gallon of gas—people go more miles, thus offsetting, at least in part, the fuel savings (Moore 1991). Autos are now much smaller than they were two decades ago, so large families or groups of more than 4 or 5 individuals must often use more than one vehicle for outings, again boosting petroleum use.

Setting rigid standards is virtually always inefficient, likely to inflate costs, and rarely productive of much gain. In the 1970s, for example, Congress amended the Clean Air Act—ostensibly to reduce air pollution—to protect coal miners in the Midwest by forcing new power plants to burn local "dirty" coal but install expensive scrubbers, thus preserving the workers' jobs. As a result, power companies constructed few new plants but maintained the old ones, which were highly polluting, long past their expected lifetime. It is easier to believe in little green men from Mars than in Congress's acting to put coal miners out of work now to protect people 100 years hence from warm weather. Unfortunately, Congress could be stampeded into adopting a regulatory scheme that would be inefficient, ineffective, unnecessary, and costly but that did not obviously endanger jobs.

Even if no-regrets policies were effective in reducing energy use, they would fail to stem the buildup of greenhouse gases. Reductions of greenhouse gases by any one nation are unlikely to have a significant effect on world emissions overall, so an international agreement by the major industrialized countries and a large number of the larger rapidly growing economies, such as China and India, would be requisite for slowing potential warming. Those countries view growth as more important than stabilizing CO_2 emissions. Still other countries may see benefits from a warmer climate.

The political juggernaut, however, is already rolling. Under the Berlin Mandate, signed in 1995, the major countries of the world agreed to negotiate a treaty to reduce greenhouse gases below 1990 levels by some time in the next century. In December 1997 in Kyoto, Japan, over 150 countries met for 10 days to agree on a protocol that would curb emissions. Even though President Bill Clinton and the U.S. Congress asserted that China and other major Third World states must be included, the restrictions on CO_2 negotiated in Kyoto apply only to the rich nations of the world.

The Administration's Proposal

In the summer of 1996, Timothy Wirth, undersecretary of state for global affairs, proposed that the nations of the world make a legally binding commitment to trim greenhouse gas emissions. In January 1997, the State Department recommended that each industrialized country create an "emissions budget" that would set a level of allowable carbon dioxide emissions. An international regulator would fix the level of emissions permitted after the year 2005. The United States advocated that each member of the Organization for Economic Cooperation and Development (OECD) "ensure that its net anthropogenic emissions of greenhouse gases do not exceed its emissions budget for any applicable budget period." In other words, the administration, which opposes a constitutional amendment to balance the fiscal budget, proposed that the developed world adopt a treaty to balance an emissions budget.

A draft of the Clinton administration's plan shows that it would have, in effect, taxed carbon at $100 per ton, enough, staffers said, to cut U.S. emissions to 1990 levels. That tax implied new gasoline levies of 26¢ a gallon, a charge of $1.49 per 1,000 cubic feet of natural gas, an impost of $52.50 on each ton of coal, and a $0.02 boost in taxes on a kilowatt of electricity (*Wall Street Journal* July 15, 1997). Those charges would produce revenues of about $180 billion per year. The tax sounds familiar. Early in its first term, the Clinton administration proposed a British thermal unit (Btu) tax. Such a tax would be the liberals' dream—almost unlimited additional government revenues to spend on new projects—and the economy's nightmare of rising unemployment and slower economic progress. Moreover, economists such as Gary Yohe of Wesleyan University and Lawrence Horwitz of DRI/McGraw-Hill report that even $100 per ton would not be enough to bring emissions back to 1990 levels (Horwitz 1995; Yohe 1996).

Sensitive to its political unpopularity, the administration quickly disavowed its proposal. In a period when Congress had been weighing the repeal of the 1993 4.3-cent increase in the federal gas tax, legislators were as likely to vote to boost fuel prices significantly as to give up free parking at National Airport. Even if such a tax were imposed in the future, raising hundreds of billions of dollars per year, would the government recycle the funds? Spend them? Or waste them?

Shortly before the Kyoto meeting, the president, in his eagerness to take a position, announced a plan that would mandate binding curbs on carbon emissions to bring them to 1990 levels in the next 10 to 15 years (Clinton 1997). The plan entailed few details but mentioned spending $5 billion over the next five years on tax breaks to spur energy efficiency and to develop new nonfossil fuel technologies. The Europeans, already critical of the Japanese proposal to cut emissions 5 percent below 1990 levels by 2010, were even more irate when confronted with Mr. Clinton's new position. Earlier in the year, on July 25, the Senate had passed unanimously Senate Resolution 98, asserting that the United States should not sign any treaty that fails to hold developing countries to the same standards as the industrialized countries or results in serious harm to the U.S. economy. To meet this mandate, the president promised that "the United States will not assume binding obligations unless key developing nations meaningfully participate in this effort" (Clinton 1997).

The president's proposal was singularly short on specifics. In effect, the president recommended that we commit to restrictions without considering how to achieve them or what they would cost. According to the White House, under a business as usual strategy, greenhouse gas emissions would exceed 1990 levels by 30 percent in 15 years. No matter how well spent, the president's proposed expenditure of $1 billion annually for five years will not reduce those emissions to the 1990 levels. Nor can that reduction be achieved by installing 20,000 solar panels on the roofs of federal buildings. Such a drastic cut would take stronger measures than efforts to make new forms of energy, not dependent on fossil fuels, practical.

The president also proposed that reduced regulation of the electricity industry would save consumers billions of dollars while reducing greenhouse gas emissions. Those are likely to be contrary goals. If deregulation leads to lower power costs, elementary economics teaches that people will use more electricity because they will be less inclined to conserve. Only if reduced controls over the power companies improve efficiency of generation and transmission sufficiently to compensate for the more prolific use of electricity will there be any net savings in carbon emissions.

Automobiles, trucks, and other vehicles emit about one-third of all U.S. carbon dioxide. The only way to reduce emissions from such mobile sources is to impose higher fuel costs or to require new vehicles to meet more stringent fuel economy standards. Since travel would be cheaper, the latter policy would encourage more traffic, resulting in greater highway congestion. Consequently, it would save much less fuel and produce more CO_2 than expected. Moreover, more stringent CAFE standards would require years to convert the existing fleet of autos into a more fuel-efficient one and would probably fail to meet the 2012 target. If Clinton is serious about slashing emissions, the Congress would have to boost gasoline taxes sharply. Whether the administration goes the higher fuel-cost route or chooses the more stringent CAFE standards, it is certain that consumers would be forced to buy lighter, more vulnerable cars, which would increase highway deaths.

The president's plan also envisioned a market system for trading emissions, which would require that major energy producers face quotas for carbon dioxide emissions. If a power plant is limited to emitting a given amount of CO_2, it must either buy certificates to allow it to exceed that level, change its fuel, or introduce new technology. None of these options is costless and the expense would have to be passed on to consumers.

The trading scheme was presumably patterned after the program submitted in January to the international group drafting the Kyoto agreement. That draft protocol would require each country to establish multiyear budgets for greenhouse gas emissions, particularly of carbon dioxide. All OECD members, with two significant exceptions (noted below), plus those countries that were part of the former Soviet empire, including Bulgaria, Ukraine, and Russia itself, would be required to limit emissions. The collapse of the economy in Russia and in the former members of the Soviet Union makes their meeting lower CO_2 standards easy. Many of their most polluting industries either have been shut down or are operating at a fraction of their former value. Nevertheless, those countries would be faced with less stringent requirements than the advanced industrialized countries that make up the OECD. The rest of the world—China, India, all of Latin America, and Africa—would be encouraged to become signatories to the agreement but would not have to meet those standards. It is worth noting that South Korea and Mexico, new members of the OECD, have asserted that they will remain exempt from the greenhouse gas requirements.

As noted, the State Department has also proposed that compliance with the requirements be monitored by an international group of experts. Making governments enforce restrictions on their own industries would be a major problem. The benefits of curbing emissions go to the world at large but the costs are paid locally. Careful monitoring of enforcement efforts would be necessary, contentious, expensive, and difficult. In fact, international oversight would almost certainly fail.

As punishment for failing to meet the budget ceilings, the United States suggested that countries be forbidden to sell carbon equivalent certificates (an empty threat since a state not in compliance would presumably have no emissions credits to sell) or that they lose voting rights in the Convention, a penalty that would certainly keep world leaders up at night! While the United States would be likely to abide by any agreement, compliance by other states is less assured.

Other Proposals

European nations recommended a carbon or an energy tax to curtail CO_2 production to 15 percent below 1990 levels by the year 2010. Although no one knows exactly how high taxes would have to be to achieve such a level of emissions reduction, a carbon tax of several hundred dollars per ton would have to be levied to reduce fossil fuel use significantly. The European Union proposal would have required Germany and a few other member countries to curb emissions by at least 25 to 30 percent while some nations, such as Portugal, could have increased their release of greenhouse gases by up to 40 percent.

The OECD has also floated a proposal to tax aviation fuel used on international flights and hitherto untaxed. The report recommends that the tax be boosted gradually over time. Needless to say, the airline industry strongly opposes this proposal. As it points out, CO_2 emissions from commercial aircraft account for only 2 percent of all such output. Such a tax would affect all international air travelers, depress tourism, and discourage trade. It would also boost unemployment, slow growth, and encourage isolationism.

Australia and Japan, among others, wanted different emissions reduction requirements for each of the advanced countries. Australia, which relies on the sale of fossil fuels abroad and has no nuclear power, wanted its dependence on coal taken into account. Heavily populated Japan proposed setting emissions limits on a per capita basis, which would have adversely affected sparsely settled Australia. The Japanese proposed a 5 percent cut from 1990 levels but with different requirements depending on the national economy. (They wound up with a 6 percent reduction.) Oil-producing nations as well as those with extensive coal reserves opposed any legally binding constraints on burning fossil fuels.

The World Debate

The politics of warming involves both domestic considerations and international agreements. Domestically, politicians compete to demonstrate their commitment to *saving the planet* while continuing to protect favored industries and groups. To cite but one example, coal miners in the U.S. have demonstrated their political clout in clean air battles. Realizing the potential consequences, the AFL-CIO has come out strongly against any treaty that does not impose equal restraints on Third World countries. The U.S. Senate has unanimously passed a nonbinding resolution against any agreement that does not include China, India, Mexico, and Brazil.

On the world scene, conferences and pronouncements abound. At the end of June 1997, world leaders gathered in New York for what was dubbed "Rio plus Five" but became known as "Rio minus Five." President Clinton was charged by some of our closest allies with failing to lead the world. Although the president gave a rousing speech, painting a fearsome picture of a world full of storms, rising seas, and spreading disease, he feared more the wrath of the voters than the wrath of the weather or of his colleagues.

The new British prime minister, Tony Blair, the German chancellor, Helmut Kohl, and President Jacques Chirac of France took the United States to task for failing to adopt stringent goals on greenhouse gas emissions. On the other hand, the Australian government was pleased that the United States did not endorse the European Union plan to cut greenhouse gas emissions over the next 12 years by more than 15 percent. The Canadians, Japanese, and Scandinavians seemed more on the fence. What was going on?

Figure 6-1
ECONOMIC GROWTH RATES OVER LAST FIVE YEARS

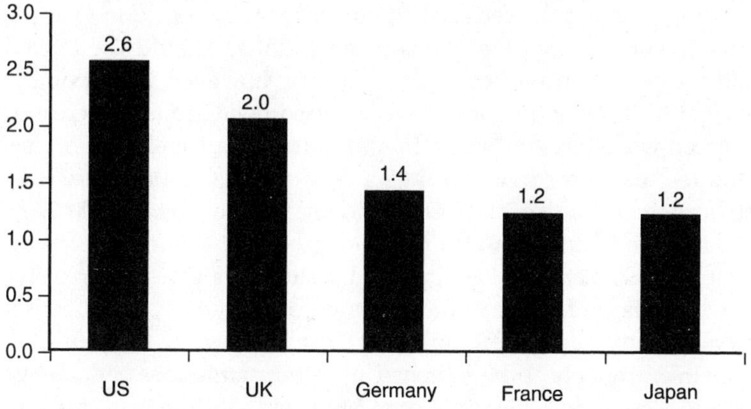

SOURCE: *Economic Report to the President*, 1997.

Why should the British and the Germans have pushed such drastic steps when, as pointed out above, the result would be devastating to their energy-intensive industries? In part, their politicians could pose as "greens," knowing full well that the United States will never agree to such restrictions. Moreover, since European Union emissions have grown much less than have those originating in North America, meeting the standards would be less costly to those states than to the United States. In fact, both Germany and the United Kingdom have actually cut their emissions of greenhouse gases in the 1990s, making them feel morally superior and able to lecture the wasteful Americans.

Two factors have contributed to less greenhouse gas emissions from the European Union. As Figure 6-1 shows, the United Kingdom, Germany, France, and Japan have all grown much more slowly than the United States over the last five years. Slow growth means less energy use and, hence, more modest increases in CO_2 emissions. In addition, with the fall of the Berlin Wall, the West Germans took over the communist East, which had been populated with inefficient, coal-burning industries. Those plants could not compete with the modern facilities in the West. Even though the Bonn government attempted to maintain industry in the former Marxist East (primarily to protect jobs), much of the industry was so hopelessly inefficient that it was eventually shut down. The resulting reduction in CO_2 emissions has put the Federal Republic in a strong position to argue that, since it has met the obligations of Rio, so should the United States. Opposition parties in that country, however, have pointed out that the area of the former West Germany has, in fact, increased its greenhouse gas emissions. In addition, the European Union has admitted that, were it not for the halving of East German emissions, the European Union's total CO_2 would rise 9 percent by the year 2000.

The United Kingdom also has undergone considerable readjustment. The Conservative government instituted a privatization program for its inefficient, money-losing coal industry. As a consequence, many mines were forced to close. That was a one-time cut, of course, unlikely to be matched by future emissions reductions. Nevertheless, it has allowed Prime Minister Blair to reproach President Clinton for the U.S. failure to curb its greenhouse gases.

Although the French might have to make significant reductions in carbon dioxide emissions to meet the European goal, they joined the other European Union countries in attacking the United States. Anything that might slow the U.S. boom, reflected in a less than 5 percent unemployment rate in comparison with more than twice that level for France and Germany, is worth the costs to the anti-American Gaullists. Meeting the European proposal would reduce U.S. competitiveness compared with that of the Europeans. Moreover, as President Chirac remarked pointedly at the G-7 summit, "The average American is responsible for emitting three times the amount of greenhouse gas as the average Frenchman." The relatively low levels of French emissions result from that country's reliance on nuclear energy for 80 percent of its power and the taxing of gasoline at rates that, if imposed in the United States, would make blood flow on the streets of American cities and towns.

On the other side of the issue were the Australians, who rely exclusively on fossil fuels for energy and who also export large quantities of coal. Prime Minister John Howard has asserted that a flat-rate reduction in emissions would devastate the Australian economy. He said recently: "We're a net exporter of energy and we're a highly developed country and if the current European and American proposals go through, it will damage Australia, cost Australian jobs, reduce our GDP. . . ." He wanted any agreement to provide "differentiated" goals that take into account each country's special circumstances, particularly its reliance on fossil fuels. The minister for foreign affairs, Alexander Downer, affirmed in July 1997 that the European Union's target for reducing its greenhouse gas emissions by 15 percent by 2010 was "unworkable" and "unacceptable" (Downer 1997).

Within the United States, politicians, experts, and academics were split on the issue. Pushing the administration to agree to the European standards or, at least, to rigid limits, were environmentalists, a handful of politicians, and some well-meaning commentators. On the other side were those concerned with any agreement's impact on economic growth, employment, and trade; those who are skeptical about the significance of any climate change; and those who find evidence that a warmer world would on balance prove beneficial.

Nor is the debate an entirely partisan affair. Representative John Dingell, a senior Democratic member of the U.S. House of Representatives Commerce Committee, has repeatedly requested that the administration provide an economic analysis of the effects of any agreement. That analysis has yet to appear. Representative Dingell is particularly concerned with the exemption from stringent controls of developing countries, such as China and India. This powerful Michigan representative fears, with some justice, that the Kyoto agreement will be costly and will potentially result in an "economic fiasco."

The Kyoto Agreement

The outcome of Kyoto remained uncertain until the morning of the eleventh day, after the scheduled ending of the Conference of Parties, Third Session. The cleaning people were getting the hall ready for the next convention and some of the Russian translators had already left. The agreement reached reflected almost a total capitulation on the part of the United States.

By the time Vice President Gore arrived on Monday, after a week of gridlock, the Conference had degenerated into a mix of revival meeting and guerrilla warfare. One night a group held a prayer meeting around the ice sculptures, pleading for their forgiveness as they began to melt. The Korean Federation of Environment Movements put signs on bushes outside the entrance proclaiming "Cool the Earth, Save Us," "Reduce GHGs [greenhouse gases] 20%,"

"Please: Gas Masks!" "Silent but Angry," "No Nukes, No Fossil Fuel for Us." (No Energy?) Given that CO_2 fertilizes plants, that research has shown that 95 percent of all plants would grow faster, bigger, and would utilize water more efficiently in a world enriched with carbon dioxide, the KFEM's "Know Nothing" position was stunning. On the last day, a Japanese environmental group organized a demonstration in behalf of forests. The trees, too, were against CO_2!

Another group of environmentalists demonstrated against air travel; I assume they wanted us to go home by ship, preferably by sailboat. Greenpeace mounted a humongous solar-powered kitchen, with an environmentally friendly refrigerator, powered by $20,000 worth of solar panels, jutting 15 feet into the air—something all housewives hunger for. To offset the somewhat pricey cooler, they offered free solar-brewed coffee, at least when the sun was shining. Greenpeace also exhibited a huge metal dinosaur made of scrap auto parts—at least they were recycling. I admit to being impressed with the metal reptile if not with their arguments. In keeping with the spirit of the occasion, the thermostat in the conference hall was turned down from its normal 73° to 68°, which forced many participants into wearing coats indoors. That brought many complaints but saved about 2 percent of the conference hall's heating bill—that should save the planet!

"Eco," a green publication, one of the newsletters published at the conference, reported, "It was a lovely day, rather hot for December. It seemed that climate was on our side." Now if they could take their instinctive preference for global warming and translate it into policy, we could put all of this to rest.

The foregoing rendition has barely conveyed the overwhelming fundamentalist environmental flavor of the convention. The halls were swarming with young, earnest types—vegetarian sandwiches sold out quickly at the snack bar—who were preaching the gospel of an energy-free world. Abstinence or, in modern terminology, conservation was the only road to salvation. Overheard was one young man saying to an eager female environmentalist, "You must come up and see my wind farm." Those of us who questioned the need for a treaty could be counted on one hand while those who thought that no treaty would be strong enough to save the world were legion.

On his arrival, the vice president said that he had given instructions to the U.S. delegation "to show increased negotiating flexibility if a comprehensive plan can be put in place, one with realistic targets and timetables, market mechanisms, and the meaningful participation of key developing countries."

Gore's speech fit well into the dominantly religious flavor of the Kyoto meetings. He spoke of "a fundamentally new stage in the development of human civilization." Really!! "The most vulnerable part of the Earth's environment is the very thin layer of air clinging near to the surface of the planet, that we are now so carelessly filling with gaseous wastes [CO_2, the basic food for plants] that we are actually altering the relationship between the Earth and the Sun." Oh sure!! "The extra heat which . . . is beginning to change the global patterns of climate . . . to which we have adapted over the last 10,000 years." [What about the previous 100,000 years?] Changing human behavior ". . . requires humility, because the spiritual roots of our crisis are pridefulness [Yea, brother!] and a failure to understand and respect our connections to God's Earth and to each other." Amen!! "Our children's children will read about the 'Spirit of Kyoto,' and remember well the place and time where humankind first chose to embark together on a long-term sustainable relationship between our civilization and the Earth's environment." Alleluia!! He wound up by comparing opponents of the treaty to cigarette manufacturers.

In the evening, at his press conference, Gore shifted slightly to say that "in order to send an agreement to the Senate, we must have meaningful participation." Meanwhile the Chinese had emphasized their "no, no, no" policy. "No" to any restrictions; "no" to any agreement on future restrictions; and "no" to any inclusion in the treaty of any reference to voluntary restrictions. Members of the Group of 77 (virtually all Third World countries numbering many more than 77) also echoed the Chinese position.

The Europeans held out for more stringent cutbacks than Clinton had proposed. As a result, the American delegation agreed to reduce U.S. emissions 7 percent by the commitment period, 2008 to 2012. The Third World countries were not even mentioned in the document. Other advanced countries have targets ranging from an 8 percent cut (the European Union) to an allowed 10 percent increase for Iceland. The reductions are to be applied to the carbon dioxide equivalent emissions of carbon dioxide, methane, and nitrous oxide and are cutbacks from 1990 outputs. For hydrofluorocarbons, perfluorocarbons, and sulphur hexafluoride, the limits are to be calculated from 1995 emissions.* The negotiators failed to agree on any enforcement mechanism or sanctions for noncompliance. The United States did win (if that is the right term) the right to trade emissions among developed countries, subject to review at the next meeting, and, in a separate agreement, an exemption for "multilateral operations" approved by the United Nations.

All the countries signing the protocol are required to have in place by 2007 a system for measuring manmade greenhouse gases and their removal by sinks.† But such a measuring scheme is neither easy nor very accurate. Scientists know that more carbon dioxide is absorbed by sinks worldwide than they can account for. Since climatologists do not know where all the CO_2 goes, can any country determine how much carbon dioxide is being reabsorbed domestically? Measuring the other gases will also be neither easy nor straightforward. Does anyone really believe that Ukraine, Greece, and Romania will have an accurate monitoring system in place by the start of this program?

Even if the Congress takes the issue of global warming seriously, it will have major problems with this agreement. First, its exclusion of China, India, and Brazil will badly hurt American industry and many manufacturing jobs will be exported. Given the overwhelming opposition among both Democrats and Republicans to any agreement that fails to include these countries, the prospect for Senate ratification is close to zero. Moreover, giving the United Nations— including Russia and China both of which have veto power in the Security Council—power over our military outside the United States is unlikely to be popular. In addition, the air force, navy, and armored ground forces will be constrained domestically. Will the air force, for example, be able to properly train their pilots, which requires regular and frequent flights?

Effectiveness of the Agreement

The Kyoto agreement entails forecasts of future greenhouse gas emissions. But energy use, which requires the burning of fossil fuels,

---

*The first two of these gases were developed as alternatives to chlorofluorocarbons (CFCs) banned under the 1987 Montreal Protocol. The last is used in heavy industry to insulate high-voltage equipment. All three have 140 to 23,000 times the warming potential of CO_2.

†Sinks are biological or physiological processes that remove CO_2 from the atmosphere and store it. Trees and oceans, for example, both take up carbon dioxide and convert the carbon to other forms such as wood or calcium carbonate.

depends on economic growth and prosperity. Economists are poor soothsayers and often over- or underestimate growth. Accurate forecasts for a long period are impossible. Not only are we unable to predict the economic future but technology can change greatly, leading to more or to less demand for fossil fuels. If countries levied carbon taxes, probably the most efficient method for reducing CO_2 emissions, the magnitude of their effect on demand for energy and the amount of fossil fuels consumed would be uncertain; it would depend, among other things, on the availability of substitutes, income effects, the price responsiveness of the public, and distributional consequences.

Moreover, modelers project that most of the climate change will come to pass many decades hence, with the forecasted 4.5°F temperature increase not occurring for 100 years. No one can have any reasonable idea about technology, population, or energy sources a century into the future. We can project, however, that future generations will have better technology at their disposal; that they will be wealthier; and that they will live longer. They will certainly be in a better position to deal with any adverse changes in the climate than is mankind today.

The Clinton administration had difficulty in deciding on what it could accept at Kyoto. Its quandary was magnified by the projected failure of the United States to reduce emissions to 1990 levels by the year 2000. Rather than cutting them, a booming economy appears likely to boost emissions of carbon dioxide by at least 15 percent in this decade. Meeting the goal of cutting emissions enough to prevent climate change, which might require slashing emissions by some 60 percent, seems out of reach. Avoiding a warmer world would require a radical curbing of emissions by all countries, which in turn would lead to a worldwide slowdown in growth, perhaps even a depression that might make the 1930s look like Disneyland on a good day.

The Kyoto agreement is futile. Even the former chairman of the IPCC, Bert Bolin, says that the present plan would, if fully implemented, cut warming 25 years hence "by less than 0.1 degree C, which would not be detectable" (Bolin 1997). We are plunging into the treaty process without even preparing an evaluation of the costs and benefits of doing so. The Congress has demanded that the Clinton administration provide them with figures on what might be the cost to the American people of the agreement, but no estimates have been forthcoming.

The Clinton administration has promised that no energy taxes are being planned. The most likely result will be a costly regulatory scheme designed to hide the deleterious effects of curbing energy consumption. Attempting to suppress the use of fossil fuels would be extraordinarily expensive and would reduce world growth significantly. The result would be mounting unemployment around the globe. Deprived of the prospect of rising incomes, the poor would feed unrest, exacerbating radical movements of all kinds. Violence would escalate. Countries buffeted between domestic demands for cheap energy and international pressures to slash the use of fossil fuels would cheat and avoid meeting treaty goals.

According to a Charles River Associates study, a cut of 10 percent from 1990 levels by the year 2030—a little more than was agreed to—would lower real national incomes from 3 to 4.5 percent in Canada, the United States, and Japan (Bernstein et al. 1997). Although Germany and the United Kingdom would be the least affected among the advanced countries, each would lose over 1.5 percent of its GDP by 2030. Oil- and coal-exporting countries also would suffer, since demand for fossil fuels by OECD countries would fall, reducing world energy prices. This study did find some winners: Jordan, Panama, South Korea, the Sudan, the Philippines, India, and Brazil, among others. Those countries gain because their emissions remain unconstrained and they are not energy producers but energy importers. Moreover, they export energy-intensive goods that would benefit from lower real prices of fossil fuels. Even those winners might lose if the wealthy countries of the world should resort to trade protection to save their energy-intensive industries from the competition of exempt Third World states. Unfortunately, given the combination of organized labor and American industries that would suffer, protectionist policies appear to be a very likely result and would aggravate any worldwide decline in incomes, doubling the loss for Asian, Latin American, and African countries.

An Australian study finds a somewhat different pattern of losses (Fisher 1997). All the OECD countries would lose; but Australia, New Zealand, and Japan would suffer the largest drops in per capita income. A 10 percent cut in emissions by Canada and the United States would reduce incomes for every man, woman, and child by roughly $1,700 to $2,000; a family of four might lose $8,000 annually. The 7 percent cut would reduce that family's earnings by $5,600 per year. The European Union would suffer less. With the exception of South Korea, most Third World countries also would lose. With tradable quotas, the Australian paper finds that losses would be smaller and that the countries that made up the former Soviet Union and Eastern Europe would actually benefit from the sale of CO_2 reduction certificates. They would profit because their heavy, energy- intensive industry has collapsed, thus giving them large quotas of reduced carbon dioxide emissions to sell. In contrast, the United States will suffer a greater loss under tradable quotas than under fixed cutbacks, because its competitors in the world market will actually gain more than the United States, thus reducing the relative competitiveness of American industry.

If they ever agree to cutbacks in greenhouse gas emissions, which they would be unlikely to meet, many poor countries would require large handouts. Environmentalists would urge governments to punish countries that failed to cut back on energy use by imposing trade restrictions. Labor and industry would argue that it was unfair for firms facing much higher energy costs to compete with companies in areas not subject to restrictions; these firms in exempt states would be benefiting from reductions in fossil fuel prices. As mentioned above, the United States, Japan, and the European Union, to protect their energy-using industries, will likely impose import controls. Restrictions on foreign trade would precipitate a downward spiral in global income that could easily produce a worldwide depression. The consumers of the country imposing the restrictions would suffer from higher prices and inferior products. Under this dreary scenario, the result would be greater world poverty. Everyone would be a loser.

Moreover, unless India and China agree to cut their future emissions, any U.S. reduction in greenhouse gases will be largely fruitless. By 2050, the UN predicts that Third World countries, exempt from controls under current agreements, would emit three-quarters of all CO_2 emissions (National Center for Policy Analysis 1996). Reducing employment and incomes in the United States would do little to stave off any climate change but would give a significant relative economic advantage to the emerging economies of Asia. Notwithstanding their relative gain, the drop in GDP in the United States, Japan, and Europe may cut Western imports and consequently reduce Asian incomes as well.

The Costs of Acting

The costs of either the tax or the emissions certificates would depend on the levels imposed. Holding CO_2 emissions constant at some level, such as the output of 1990, or cutting emissions in the developed world by 5 percent (the Kyoto goal), would only slow the buildup of CO_2. To stabilize concentrations of CO_2 in the atmosphere at levels equal to or below twice the pre-Industrial Revolution concentration would require major cuts from 1990 emissions for the world as a whole. Even reducing emissions that far would not stabilize global temperatures until the 22nd century.

DRI/McGraw-Hill, a respected consulting firm, calculated that the government would have to exact taxes of $100 to $200 per ton of carbon to trim U.S. emissions to 1990 levels by the year 2010, depressing GDP by 2.3 to 4.2 percent—roughly $1,700 to $3,100 per household—with the higher estimate being more than twice the amount spent by the government and the private sector together on all other environmental issues (Horwitz 1995). If the tax were only $100, and assuming that the revenues were recycled through lump sum cuts in personal income taxes, Lawrence Horwitz, who carried out the research, calculates that the real GDP of the United States would drop by 2.3 percent and about half a million jobs would be lost each year while the tax was being phased in. A peak loss of about 1 million would occur two years after the tax was fully implemented (Horwitz 1995). But probably more damning are the inequities of such a policy. The cost would be borne by all consumers, yet only income tax payers, who are the higher income consumers, would receive the rebate.

But even that major effort would only slow the growth of greenhouse gases in the atmosphere. Actually stabilizing the concentration of gases in the atmosphere would require losses to the economy of several times DRI's projections. Given political pressures to protect certain industries and some favored consumers, costs could well exceed even those staggering numbers.

Although no one can be certain of the burden, most respectable estimates indicate that the cost would be staggering. Yale's William Nordhaus, whose work was discussed in the previous chapter, concluded that the net discounted cost to the world of meeting the Rio agreement's goal of 1990 levels would be $7 trillion—about the total of the United States' annual GDP (Nordhaus 1994, 82). This mind-blowing figure represents the cost to the world in excess of his estimate of the benefits from reduced warming! Moreover, returning to 1990 emission levels would fail to prevent a buildup of greenhouse gases; according to the models it would only slow climate change.

Gary Yohe of Wesleyan University estimates that it would cost $260 per ton of carbon to reduce CO_2 to 1990 levels by 2010 and would lower the growth rate of GDP by one percentage point annually. Income and wages would drop 5 to 10 percent per year (Yohe 1996). Gas prices would soar about 75 cents a gallon while heating oil prices would more than double. Low-income families may have to choose between cold cuts and a cold house. All these predicted costs envision a less stringent program than agreed to at Kyoto. The costs also assume that the government imposes the most efficient scheme to slash emissions—taxes or emission certificates.

No matter which scheme is adopted to limit greenhouse gas emissions, the United States will be a loser. Restrictions on energy use in the United States will hurt our industries, especially those that are energy intensive, such as the auto industry, the coal and oil industries, the steel industry, and transportation generally. The cost of the programs will be reflected in every item bought in the supermarket. Every home in the country will pay more for electricity, hot water, heating, and air conditioning.

As indicated, only the OECD countries have committed themselves to abide fully by any restrictions; the Third World states remain free to develop their economies in any way they see fit. Supposedly, those countries that had been part of the Soviet empire—Eastern and Central Europe—will also have to limit their production of CO_2, but they face less stringent requirements that, given their weak economies, will probably be waived. As a consequence, our industry and our economy will bear the brunt of the agreement.

The industries that are particularly vulnerable to higher energy costs will be tempted to move abroad, to parts of the world not subject to controls. Although Ross Perot was wrong when he said that NAFTA would produce a sucking sound as jobs moved south, one can hear echoes of that noise emanating from these agreements. As the AFL-CIO said in its February 20, 1997 statement: "The exclusion of new commitments by developing nations under the Berlin Mandate will create a powerful incentive for transnational corporations to export jobs, capital, and pollution, and will do little or nothing to stabilize atmospheric concentrations of carbon. Such an uneven playing field will cause the loss of high-paying U.S. jobs in the mining, manufacturing, transport, and other sectors."

The Clinton administration's own Department of Energy (DOE) reports that attempting to comply with any of these scenarios would be disastrous for American industry. To study the potential impact of the restrictions on energy-intensive industries, the DOE commissioned a study by the Argonne National Laboratory. The resulting paper focused on six sectors: chemicals, petroleum refining, paper and allied products, iron and steel, aluminum, and cement (Sutherland 1997). To model the effect of policies designed to reduce greenhouse gas emissions, the researchers added a premium to the prices of fossil fuels based on their carbon content. Carried out before the last election, when tax increases were not considered "politically correct," the study assumed that the price of the fuels would be uplifted magically without hiking taxes. The nontax add-ons to fuel costs, dubbed "price adders," had the effect of boosting electricity rates by slightly more than 50 percent from the year 2000 to 2010, tripling coal prices, inflating natural gas charges by about 80 percent, and pushing up fuel oil costs between 70 and 90 percent.

The department's research team at Argonne found that "the policy constraints placed on these six large industries in developed countries, but not on their less developed trading partners, would result in significant adverse impacts on the affected industries." The study went on to emphasize that "furthermore, GHG [GreenHouse Gas] emissions would not be reduced significantly. . . . Price increases based on carbon content, [are] neither effective, nor cost-effective in encouraging a reduction in GHG emissions. Some substitutions encouraged by fuel price increases could actually increase GHG emissions."

To conduct the study, the Argonne National Laboratory established six working groups, one for each of the six industrial sectors, consisting of eight or nine experts from industry, trade associations, environmental groups, academe, the financial community, labor unions, and the government. The conclusions of all six groups were surprisingly consonant and gloomy. The working group on iron and steel, for example, stated categorically:

> The imposition of increased energy costs will devastate the U.S. steel industry without a significant decrease in worldwide energy related emissions from steel making. Production

will simply be shifted to developing countries and may possibly lead to higher levels of overall pollution due to lower standards in those countries.

The Petroleum Refining Industry working group emphasized that

[the] application of add-factors [taxes or imposed costs] on OECD refiner production (or crude input) would devastate and probably eliminate the OECD refining sectors. Moreover, the resulting realignment of supply into non-OECD regions ... would probably not cut and would probably raise net GHG emissions from the global petroleum supply industry.

Each of the working groups found that higher energy outlays would boost the cost of production, lead to increased imports, and slash employment and domestic output. In some cases, higher energy costs might eliminate all U.S. production. The groups also agreed that the "policy scenarios would not produce a reduction in global emissions and these emissions could actually increase." The study concluded that employment in the steel industry would fall by about 65 percent, meaning that about 80,000 highly paid workers would lose their jobs. Employment in cement would be slashed by one-third. The United States would have to sacrifice its entire primary aluminum industry, abolishing all 21,000 jobs and liquidating an industry essential to American security.

The conclusion of the DOE report is worth quoting at length:

Higher fuel costs imposed on domestic energy intensive industries would result in an increase in production costs in these industries. The consensus of the six working groups ... is that imports from nonparticipating countries would displace a significant amount of U.S. industrial output and employment. A substantial amount of existing capacity in several of these industries would become noncompetitive. Future investment in plant and equipment would be redirected from the United States ... towards nonparticipating countries. *This conclusion is more general: all participating countries that agree to binding constraints will experience an economic decline relative to nonparticipating countries* (Sutherland 1997, 21, emphasis added).

Although the DOE study concentrated only on major industries, the public should be aware of the effect on daily life of mandatory

149

restrictions on greenhouse gas emissions. The price increases necessitated by the agreement would inflate the cost of virtually everything they buy, leaving consumers much worse off. If fuel oil goes up by 70 to 90 percent, the price of gasoline at the pump will rise—before taxes—a comparable amount, roughly 50 to 60 cents per gallon. Trucking costs will go up roughly 12 percent, making everything the housewife buys more costly.

The Tradeoff

The previous chapter indicated that the effects of global warming would probably be positive for the United States and for much of the rest of the world. At most, in a hundred years (assuming the most pessimistic view), climate change might impose costs of around 1 to 2 percent of world GDP. The cost of preventing a buildup of greenhouse gases would be much larger than even the darkest estimates of a warmer world. True, a few poor countries might suffer from rising sea levels or be unable to adjust their agriculture and so would suffer significantly. If emission controls are intended to protect those countries, then this kind of foreign aid might be better targeted to promoting their economic development. Since the cost of slowing warming exceeds the projected benefits by a substantial margin, however, the right strategy is to do nothing, except perhaps to help poor countries improve their economies. That way there will be no regrets.

As mentioned, Bert Bolin, former chairman of the IPCC, in the IPCC Report to the Ad Hoc Group on the Berlin Mandate, concluded that "no reasonable future reductions by Annex I countries [OECD and countries in transition to a market economy] would stabilize global emissions." Is it reasonable to cut our GDP by 2 or 3 percent, or maybe even more, when the best that could be accomplished would be to shave the average global temperature by less than 0.1 degree Celsius (0.2°F)? Should the United States and other OECD countries decimate their aluminum, steel, chemical, oil refining, paper, and cement industries for such a paltry outcome?

Even in the unlikely event that all countries around the globe agreed to cap CO_2 emissions at levels that would prevent warming— some 50 percent or 60 percent below current emissions—the gain would be small or nonexistent while the cost would be staggering. If returning emissions to 1990 levels would cost the economy of the

United States and the world somewhere around 2.5 to 3.5 percent of income, slashing emissions well below that would be catastrophic. Fortunately, since most people will benefit from a warmer globe, such steps are unnecessary.

However, if the world were to act to cap concentrations of greenhouse gases, the cost of doing so would depend on how soon emissions were cut. Following a business-as-usual policy for the next few decades would actually be the cheapest alternative. Scientists have calculated the effects of waiting until 2010 or 2020 before capping emissions; in general, they conclude that waiting would be less costly than acting now (Wigley et al. 1996). Researchers give four reasons for delaying action: (1) an expenditure that must be made decades hence is less burdensome than outlays made now; (2) the capital stock invested in power plants, houses, and factories needs time to be amortized since such facilities are long-lived; (3) technological progress should improve the efficiency of energy supply, reducing the costs of substitute, carbon-free energy sources; (4) natural sinks absorb CO_2 emissions over time, so a larger cumulative emissions budget would be possible, reducing our dependence on higher-cost low- or no-carbon alternatives. In addition, the United States and the rest of the world would be richer a few decades hence and better, able to bear any burden from cutting carbon emissions or mitigating any harm from climate change.

Since climate change will have only a very small effect on most of the world, why are so many rushing to impose onerous taxes and controls on U.S. industry? The carbon tax that the administration suggested and then withdrew would cost Americans about $180 billion per year. Spending only one-tenth of that to provide clean water or mosquito netting would contribute far more to the world's health than attempting to reduce greenhouse gas emissions. If preventing an increase in disease in poor countries or rising seas from inundating Bangladesh is the purpose of restricting those emissions, then it would be much more effective to deal with those problems directly than to put constraints on our energy use.

A cynic might claim that the proponents of signing an agreement in Kyoto aim to force the private sector to subsidize other countries by crafting a mechanism to induce U.S. companies to purchase CO_2 rights from other nations. Given the collapse of the Soviet Union's heavy industries, Russia and other former Soviet bloc states would have ample CO_2 reductions from 1990 levels to sell to the West.

The ability to buy emission reduction certificates from Eastern Europe and perhaps from some Third World countries means that the U.S. plan would reduce emissions significantly neither in the industrialized world nor elsewhere. As a scheme to halt global warming, it is a sham. It will, however, produce a huge and expensive international bureaucracy, impose an implicit tax on industry, especially on energy-intensive industry, and significantly raise gasoline taxes, electricity costs, and heating and cooling costs for all Americans. It will cost Americans income, jobs, and prosperity. The only benefit, if you consider it a benefit, will be to extract some resources from American and European companies and transfer them to Russia, Ukraine, China, India, and Brazil. Two Brookings Institution economists estimated that the U.S. proposal of tradable certificates would require that U.S. companies spend around $27 billion or more annually to purchase the rights to emit carbon from Third World or former Soviet bloc countries (McKibbin and Wilcoxen 1997). That sum is nearly four times the U.S. government's annual budget for foreign economic aid.

Ratification of a treaty that caps U.S. emissions at a level significantly below 1990 appears to be remote. However, Clinton and Gore have been politically astute in past bargaining with the Congress and usually get their way over international negotiations. Al Gore, who boasts a reputation as a dedicated environmentalist, must deliver or lose his credibility. The administration has asserted that it will not submit the Protocol for Senate consideration until after it has secured "meaningful participation" by major developing countries. Officials hope to get China and others to agree to something in 1998 in Buenos Aires. At that point, the Congress would have to face rejecting a treaty and supposedly losing the U.S. leadership on the environment or going along with Clinton and the environmentalists, knowing that a distant future Congress would have to legislate the onerous energy taxes and stringent regulations necessary to meet the protocol's mandates. Let us hope that the public and the Congress will be able to see through this charade.

If We All Cooperate

Worldwide cooperation would be the only effective way to curb greenhouse gas emissions; but even if the advanced nations could get China, India, and Brazil to agree, would it be good policy? As indicated above, the cost of curbing emissions significantly around the globe is on the order of several percentage points of world income. The gain from slowed or avoided climate change would be much smaller. Moreover, for most people, in most of the world, a warmer world would be a better world. The only significant costs from global warming would be higher sea levels; but even these burdens would be spread out over the next 100 years, providing ample opportunity to construct dikes and take other steps to mitigate any damage.

Let us assume that the IPCC is right and that, by the year 2100, greenhouse gas concentrations in the atmosphere will rise significantly, driving up worldwide temperatures by 4.5° F. In all probability, if such a warming does take place, most people will be better off. On the other hand, if we take the pessimists' view, the costs to the United States might be as high as 1.5 percent of our GDP, although most estimates of the damage from climate change are considerably less than that figure (Chapter 5, Table 5-4). As reported earlier, however, DRI estimates the cost to Americans of reducing greenhouse gas emissions to 1990 levels as 2.3 percent of GDP, a very bad benefit/cost ratio.

The IPCC's Working Group III reviewed various estimates of GDP losses, not including DRI's, from stabilizing emissions at 1990 levels and concluded that the average projected loss would be 1.5 percent of U.S. GDP by the year 2050, with the costs increasing more or less linearly with time (IPCC 1995c, 307). The IPCC's forecast of a 4.5° increase in temperatures is for the end of the next century, not the middle (actually, they are now projecting something less than that for the year 2100). If we assume that the temperature will go up by only half as much over the next 50 years (actually, temperatures should rise more in the second half than in the first half because of lags between carbon buildup and ocean temperatures), then the cost to the United States from warming would be, at most, only 0.75 percent, meaning that the costs of holding CO_2 to 1990 levels of 1.5 percent would be twice the gain from preventing any climate change!

But the benefit/cost calculus is even worse! Returning worldwide emissions, including the United States', to 1990 levels will *not* stabilize greenhouse gas *concentrations*. Since more CO_2 will be added annually for many decades to the atmosphere than the sinks can absorb, the buildup would only slow. Consequently, temperatures would continue to go up but by less than if no steps were taken to reduce CO_2 emissions. Therefore, instead of saving the full 0.75 percent of our GDP by keeping emissions at 1990 levels, we would be saving much less, perhaps half as much or 0.375 percent of our GDP, hardly anything worth worrying about.

The Precautionary Principle

Many advocates of acting now assert that, since there is some unknown but possibly great danger, governments should, on the basis of the precautionary principle, take steps now to reduce the specter of damage. This principle is valid only if such measures in and of themselves do not impose any risks or costs. But curbing CO_2 emissions would be very costly. As has been shown above, it would reduce incomes and wealth. Moreover, since the costs of higher energy prices would be passed on to the items that all consumers buy, it would affect most adversely those with low incomes. If, as has been proposed, carbon taxes were returned through cuts in the income tax, the adverse distributional consequences would be severe. Rich people would enjoy lower taxes while poor people would pay more for goods and services. Gary Yohe has shown that the lowest quintile in the income distribution would be most severely distressed while the highest quintile would actually benefit (Yohe 1996). Alternatively, the government might keep the revenues and spend them, with foreseeable results. An increased portion of the economy being allocated by politicians would depress growth rates and increase the costs of such policies.

As many economic studies have shown, being rich is healthier; being poor shortens one's life (Chapman and Hariharan 1994; Duleep 1986). A program that reduces incomes will increase mortality. Researchers have estimated that a loss of $5 million to $10 million in U.S. GDP would lead to one extra death (Cross 1995). Assuming that the cost of reducing greenhouse gas emissions to 1990 levels—not enough to prevent climate change, only to slow it—were 1.5 percent of GDP, the loss in today's income for the United States alone would be about $120 billion. Using the more conservative estimate of the effect of income on deaths implies that about 12,000 Americans would die prematurely each year.

Rich nations also suffer less from natural disasters, especially in human lives, than do poor regions. When the Loma Prieta earthquake struck northern California, 67 people lost their lives. A year earlier, a slightly weaker earthquake ravaged Armenia with a death toll of nearly 25,000. Slowing economic growth of poor countries, as measures taken to cap CO_2 emissions would do, would mean that underdeveloped nations would remain more exposed to damage from inevitable natural disasters. Higher worldwide mortality would be the result.

In addition, higher energy costs, plus any strengthened CAFE standards, would push consumers into buying still smaller, lighter, and more dangerous autos. Although we cannot be sure how many extra highway fatalities would result, they would be in the thousands. Higher heating costs would also increase the use of insulation and more airtight buildings, reducing ventilation and trapping more air pollution indoors. Such hazardous chemicals as formaldehyde, carbon monoxide, nitrogen oxides, volatile organic compounds, and particulates would build up inside the structures. Since people spend most of their time indoors, the quality of the air in houses and offices is important to maintaining health. Without doubt the more energy-efficient structures would cause some increase in sickness and perhaps an unknown number of early deaths.

Government regulations often, if not always, have unfortunate, unintended consequences. The effort to protect the ozone layer provides a recent example. Under the Montreal Protocol, chlorofluorocarbons (CFCs) have been banned in the industrial nations and will be phased out in the rest of the world over the next decade. CFCs are relatively inert, benign, nonpoisonous substances that provide excellent cooling. Not only do the substitutes fail to work as well, they turn out to be dangerous to people's health. Scientists have confirmed that workers accidentally exposed to substitute chemicals, such as HCFC-123 and HCFC-124, have developed acute hepatitis (*Washington Post* August 22, 1997, 14A). Moreover, two other substitutes are to be banned under Kyoto for contributing to global warming. The banned CFCs, on the other hand, produced no known cases of harm to any men or women.

This analysis has been based on the IPCC's best estimate of the rise in temperatures by the end of the next century and the average expected costs to the United States of such a change. But what if the cost should turn out to be much worse than the pessimists expect? What if the costs from global warming were to be 10 times higher than the forecast? As Wilfred Beckerman has pointed out (1996, 112), this would imply that the average person's income in 2100 would be only 3.96 times higher than it is today, rather than 4.4 times higher! Would this slight reduction in future income for the world's population warrant the risk to our economy now of stringent caps? Lowering current income to slow greenhouse gas emissions also would reduce future earnings, offsetting at least partially the "savings" from reducing possible future damage stemming from climate change.

In other words, policymakers must weigh the costs of acting to slow greenhouse gas emissions against the costs of maintaining current policy. Neither is without risk, but claiming that the precautionary principle requires action to curb CO_2 is nonsense. Under the most efficient possible policy to curb CO_2, one under which all countries cooperate to reduce their emissions, people will die, growth will be slowed (leading to more damage and fatalities from naturally occurring disasters), and the poor will suffer the most. But the politicians have signed a treaty that would be even worse. It would impose these costs yet produce little in the way of curbed emissions. That is folly.

Where Are We and Where Should We Be Going?

There is no need to rush into a hasty treaty that would produce little benefit but high costs. If climate change becomes a real problem at some future time, many steps can be taken without crippling our economy. Ocean scientists have shown, for example, that if the seas were "fertilized" with iron filings, phytoplankton (algae) would bloom and absorb vast quantities of CO_2 (*Washington Post* October 14, 1996, A3). The minuscule plants are nutritionally starved for iron and, when provided with that metal, multiply rapidly, absorbing large amounts of carbon. Kenneth S. Johnson of Moss Landing Marine Laboratories has estimated that iron supplements might offset 15 to 20 percent of man-made carbon dioxide over the next few decades (*Washington Post* October 14, 1996, A3).

In addition, harvesting and replanting timber could sequester a good bit of carbon. Forest researchers have concluded that an active program of cropping and replanting fast-growing forests, then turning the lumber into housing and other long-term products, together with reforestation, could offset 12 to 15 percent of human greenhouse gas emissions (Moffat 1997). Those two steps—iron filings in the oceans and forest management—could by themselves do as much to slow climate change as capping greenhouse gas emissions at 1990 levels. Over the next few decades scientists may develop other strategies that do not significantly lower the world's living standards.

As mentioned, the administration is under tremendous pressure from all sides to act *now*. To keep its credibility with environmentalists, many politicians, European and Japanese leaders, and leading journals, it must take steps to cut back CO_2 emissions even if the limitations would have no benefit and would potentially impose high costs. To succeed in this high-wire act, President Clinton probably will propose new regulatory steps, such as higher fuel efficiency standards for new cars, more stringent restrictions on appliances, the mandating of strict insulation levels for new buildings, and more spending on mass transportation. Most of those regulations would be phased in slowly, that is, after President Clinton leaves office and after many of the current members of Congress retire. The actual legislation required to meet the goal might even await a future Congress. Whatever the difficulties or hurdles, the administration will negotiate some formula so that Clinton, Gore, and their supporters can claim that all the world, including China, is participating in the cutback of greenhouse gases.

All of this is unnecessary, expensive, and crippling to our economy. For most of the world, the cost of warming over the next 100 years would be either very small or an actual benefit. As noted earlier, most people in most places will be better off in a warmer world. Those poor parts of the world that might suffer the most should have help. In any case, delaying action by 20 to 30 years appears to be the only truly prudent, "no-regrets" policy. Technology will advance. Incomes in Third World countries will multiply. The world will be more capable of coping with change, whatever vicissitudes may occur. Except for those measures that make sense in any case, such as eliminating subsidies on energy and energy use, the Congress should stand fast against any steps to limit greenhouse gas emissions.

References

Ammerman, Albert J., and L. L. Cavalli–Sforza. 1984. *The Neolithic Transition and the Genetics of Populations in Europe*. Princeton, N.J.: Princeton University Press.

Anderson, Christopher. 1991. Cholera Epidemic Traced to Risk Miscalculation. *Nature* 354 (November): 255.

Anderson, Robert J. Jr. 1974. The Health Costs of Changing Macro-Climates. In *Proceedings of the Third Conference on the Climatic Impact Assessment Program*. Edited by Anthony Broderick and Thomas M. Hard. Washington: U.S. Department of Transportation, pp. 582–92.

Applegate, W. B., et al. 1981. Analysis of the 1980 Heat Wave in Memphis. *Journal of the American Geriatrics Society*, 19, 337–42.

Arrhenius, Svante. 1896. On the Influence of Carbonic Acid in the Air upon the Temperature of the Ground. *Philisophical Magazine* and *Journal of Science* (April): 237–76.

Ausubel, Jesse H. 1991. A Second Look at the Impacts of Climate Change. *American Scientists* 79 (May–June): 210–21.

———. 1994. Technical Progress and Climate Change. In *Integrated Assessment of Mitigation, Impacts, and Adaptation to Climate Change*. Edited by N. Nakicenovic et al. Laxenburg, Austria: International Institute for Applied Systems Analysis, pp. 501–12.

Baker, J. T., and L. H. Allen Jr. 1994. Assessment of the Impact of Rising Carbon Dioxide and Other Potential Climate Changes on Vegetation. *Environmental Pollution* 83, 223–35.

Bartlett, Robert. 1993. *The Making of Europe: Conquest, Colonization and Cultural Change 950–1350*. Princeton, N.J.: Princeton University Press.

Beckerman, Wilfred. 1996. *Through Green-Colored Glasses: Environmentalism Reconsidered*. Washington: Cato Institute.

Bell, Frederick W. 1974. The Economic Effects of the Consequences of Stratospheric Flight on Living Marine Resources. In *Proceedings of the Third Conference on the Climatic Impact Assessment Program*. Edited by Anthony Broderick and Thomas M. Hard. Washington: U.S. Department of Transportation, pp. 612–38.

Bentley, Charles R. 1997. Rapid Sea-Level Rise Soon from West Antarctic Ice Sheet Collapse? *Science* 275 (February 21): 1077–78.

Bernstein, Paul M., W. D. Montgomery, and T. F. Rutherford. 1997. International Impacts: The Global Distributional Impacts of Climate Change Policy. Paper prepared for a conference on The Costs of Kyoto: Climate Change Policy and Its Implications, Competitive Enterprise Institute, July 15.

Blomquist, Glenn C., Mark C. Berger, and John P. Hoehn. 1988. New Estimates of Quality of Life in Urban Areas. *American Economic Review* 78 (March): 89–107.

Bolin, Bert. 1997. IPCC Report to the Fifth Session of the SBSTA and Sixth Session of the AGBM.

Boserup, Ester. 1981. *Population and Technological Change: A Study of Long-Term Trends.* Chicago: University of Chicago Press.

Bridger, C. A., F. P. Ellis, and H. L. Taylor. 1976. Mortality in St. Louis, Missouri, during Heat Waves in 1936, 1953, 1954, 1955 and 1966. *Environmental Research* 12, 38–48.

Broccoli, Anthony J. 1994. Learning from Past Climates. *Nature* 371 (September 22): 282.

Broderick, Anthony, and Thomas M. Hard, eds. 1974. *Proceedings of the Third Conference on the Climatic Impact Assessment Program.* Conference held at DOT Transportation System Center February 26–March 1. Washington: U.S. Department of Transportation. DOT-TSC-OST-74-15.

Browne, Malcolm W. 1997. South Pole Gets Colder. *New York Times, Science Times* (August 26): B11.

Bull, G. M., and Joan Morton. 1978. Environment, Temperature and Death Rates. *Age and Ageing* 7, 210–24.

Carpenter, R. 1966. *Discontinuity in Greek Civilization.* Cambridge: Cambridge University Press.

Carruth, Gorton. 1993. *The Encyclopedia of World Facts and Dates.* New York: HarperCollins.

Chapman, Kenneth S., and Govind Hariharan. 1994. Controlling for Causality in the Link from Income to Mortality. *Journal of Risk Uncertainty* 85.

Chao, Kang. 1986. *Man and Land in Chinese History: An Economic Analysis.* Stanford, Calif.: Stanford University Press.

Cheetham, Nicolas. 1981. *Mediaeval Greece.* New Haven, Conn.: Yale University Press.

Claiborne, Robert. 1970. *Climate, Man, and History.* New York: W. W. Norton.

Climate Research Unit (CRU), University of East Anglia and Environmental Resources Limited (ERL). 1992. *Development of a Framework for the Evaluation of Policy Options to Deal with the Greenhouse Effect: Economic Evaluation of Impacts and Adaptive Measures in the European Community, Report for the Commission of European Communities.* London.

Cline, William. 1992. *The Economics of Global Warming.* Washington: Institute for International Economics.

Clinton, William J. 1993. Remarks at the White House Conference on Climate Change, October 19.

———. 1997. Remarks by the President on Global Climate Change, National Geographic Society, October 22.

Cogan, Douglas. 1992. *The Greenhouse Gambit: Business and Investment Responses to Climate Change.* Washington: Investor Responsibility Center.

Cohen, Mark Nathan. 1977. *The Food Crisis in Prehistory: Overpopulation and the Origins of Agriculture.* New Haven, Conn.: Yale University Press.

———. 1989. *Health and the Rise of Civilization.* New Haven, Conn.: Yale University Press.

Colwell, Rita R. 1996. Global Climate and Infectious Disease: The Cholera Paradigm. *Science* 274 (December 20): 2025–31.

Cook, Edward, et al. 1991. Climatic Changes in Tasmania Inferred from a 1089-Year Tree Ring Chronology of Huon Pine. *Science* 253 (September 13): 1266–68.

Crandall, Robert W., and John D. Graham. 1989. The Effect of Fuel Economy Standards on Automobile Safety. *Journal of Law and Economics* 32 (April): 97–118.

Cropper, M. L. 1981. The Value of Urban Amenities. *Journal of Regional Science* 21, no. 3, 359–74.

References

Cropper, M. L., and A. S. Arriaga-Salinas. 1980. Inter-city Wage Differentials and the Value of Air Quality. *Journal of Urban Economics* 8, 236–54.

Cross, Frank B. 1995. When Environmental Regulations Kill. *Ecology Law Quarterly.*

Crowley, Thomas J. 1993. Use and Misuse of the Geologic "Analogs" Concept. In *Global Changes in the Perspective of the Past.* Edited by J. A. Eddy and H. Oeschger. Somerset, N.J.: John Wiley and Sons.

Crowley, Thomas J., and Gerald North. 1991. *Paleoclimatology.* New York: Oxford University Press.

Danzig, David. 1995. Global Warming—Health Hazard. Sierra Club.

D'Arge, Ralph C. 1974. Economic Impact of Climate Change: Introduction and Overview. In *Proceedings of the Third Conference on the Climatic Impact Assessment Program.* Edited by Anthony Broderick and Thomas M. Hard. Washington: U.S. Department of Transportation, pp. 564–74.

Davis, R. E., and S. R. Benkovic. 1994. Spatial and Temporal Variations of the January Circumpolar Vortex over the Northern Hemisphere. *International Journal of Climatology* 14, 415–28.

Deland, Antoinette. 1987. *Fielding's Far East.* New York: Fielding Travel Books.

Donkin, R. A. 1973. Changes in the Early Middle Ages. In *A New Historical Geography of England.* Edited by H. C. Darby. Cambridge: Cambridge University Press.

Downer, Alexander. 1997. Australia and Climate Change. Address to the Global Emissions Agreements and Australian Business Seminar, Melbourne, July 7.

Duleep, Harriet O. 1986. Measuring the Effect of Income on Adult Mortality Using Longitudinal Administrative Record Data. *Journal of Human Resources* 238.

Eaton, Robert. 1997. Letter to the editor. *Washington Post,* August 20.

Ellis, F. P. 1972. Mortality from Heat Illness and Heat-Aggravated Illness in the United States. *Environmental Research* 5, 1–58.

Fairbridge, R. W. 1984. The Nile Floods as a Global Climatic/Solar Proxy. In *Climatic Changes on a Yearly to Millennial Basis: Geological, Historical and Instrumental Records.* Edited by N. A. Morner and W. Karlen. Boston: Dordrecht.

Fisher, Brian. 1997. The Economic Impact of International Climate Change Policy. Paper prepared for conference on The Costs of Kyoto: Climate Change Policy and Its Implications. Competitive Enterprise Institute, July 15.

Flohn, H. 1983. A Climate Feedback Mechanism Involving Oceanic Upwelling, Atmospheric CO_2 and Water Vapour. In *Variations in the Global Water Budget.* Edited by Alayne Street-Perrott, Max Beran, and Robert Ratcliffe. Boston: D. Reidel.

Folland, C. K., et al. 1992. Observed Climate Variability and Change. In *Climate Change 1992: The Supplementary Report to the IPCC Scientific Assessment.* Edited by J. T. Houghton, B. A. Callander, and S. K. Varney. Cambridge: Cambridge University Press.

Frankhauser, S. 1995. *Valuing Climate Change: The Economics of the Greenhouse.* London: Earthscan.

Frenzel, B. 1993. Comparison of Interglacial Climates Regarding Space and Character. In *Global Changes in the Perspective of the Past.* Edited by J. A. Eddy and H. Oeschger. Somerset, N.J.: John Wiley and Sons.

Gates, W. L., et al. 1992. Climate Modeling, Climate Prediction and Model Validation. In *Climate Change 1992: The Supplementary Report to the IPCC Scientific Assessment.* Edited by J. T. Houghton, B. A. Callander, and S. K. Varney. Cambridge: Cambridge University Press.

Giles, Bill. 1990. *The Story of Weather.* London: Her Majesty's Stationery Office.

Gimpel, Jean. 1983. *The Cathedral Builders*. Trans. by Teresa Waugh. London: Pimlico.

Gore, Albert. 1992. *Earth in the Balance*. Boston: Houghton Mifflin.

Graves, Philip E. 1980. Migration and Climate. *Journal of Regional Science* 20, no. 2, 227–37.

Graves, Philip E., and Donald M. Waldman. 1991. Multimarket Amenity Compensation and the Behavior of the Elderly. *American Economic Review* 81 (December): 1374–81.

Gyourko, Joseph, and Joseph Tracy. 1991. The Structure of Local Public Finance and the Quality of Life. *Journal of Political Economy* 99 (August): 774–806.

Healy, Melissa. 1994. Gore: Global Warming Earth's Most Serious Problem. *Los Angeles Times*, April 21.

Hoch, Irving, with Judith Drake. 1974. Wages, Climate, and the Quality of Life. *Journal of Environmental Economics and Management* 1, 268–96.

Hoch, Irving. 1977. Variations in the Quality of Urban Life among Cities and Regions. In *Public Economics and the Quality of Life*. Edited by Lowdon Wingo and Alan Evans. Baltimore: Johns Hopkins University Press.

Horwitz, Lawrence M. 1995. The Impact of Carbon Dioxide Emission Reductions on Living Standards and Lifestyles. Special Report, American Council for Capital Formation, Center for Policy Research, October.

Huggett, Richard John. 1991. *Climate, Earth Processes and Earth History*. New York: Springer-Verlag.

Innes, J. L. 1994. Climatic Sensitivity of Temperate Forests. *Environmental Pollution* 83, 237–43.

Intergovernmental Panel on Climate Change. 1990. *Climate Change. The IPCC Scientific Assessment*. Edited by J. T. Houghton, G. J. Jenkins, and J. J. Ephraums. Cambridge: Cambridge University Press.

———. 1992. *The Supplementary Report to the IPCC Scientific Assessment*. Prepared by Working Group I and edited by J. T. Houghton, B. A. Callander, and S. K. Varney. Cambridge: Cambridge University Press.

———. 1995a. *The Economic and Social Dimensions of Climate Change*. Prepared by Working Group III and edited by James P. Bruce, Hoesung Lee, and Erik F. Haites. Cambridge: Cambridge University Press.

———. 1995b. *Second Assessment Report, Summary for Policy Makers: Impacts, Adaptation and Mitigation Options*. Prepared by Working Group II. Montreal.

———. 1995c. *Summary for Policy Makers: The Economic and Social Dimensions of Climate Change*. Prepared by Working Group III.

———. 1995d. *Summary for Policy Makers: The Science of Climate Change*. Prepared by Working Group I.

———. 1995e. *Global Climate Change*. Summary of IPCC Special Report on the work of the Berlin Conference, March 28–April 7. At http://www. globalchange.org/.

———. 1996. *Scientific-Technical Analyses of Impacts, Adaptations, and Mitigation of Climate Change*. Vol. 2 of *Climate Change 1995: IPCC Second Assessment Report*. Prepared by Working Group II. Cambridge: Cambridge University Press.

Journal of the American Medical Association. 1996. January 17.

Justus, John R., and Wayne A. Morrissey. 1995. *Global Climate Change*. Congressional Research Service, Report to Congress, updated November 15.

Kalkstein, Laurence S. 1991. A New Approach to Evaluate the Impact of Climate on Human Mortality. *Environmental Health Perspectives* 96, 145–50.

References

_____. 1992. Impact of Global Warming on Human Health: Heat Stress-Related Mortality. In *Global Climate Change: Implications, Challenges and Mitigation Measures*. Edited by S. K. Majumdar et al. Easton: Pennsylvania Academy of Science.

Kalkstein, Laurence S., and Robert E. Davis. 1989. Weather and Human Mortality: An Evaluation of Demographic and Interregional Responses in the United States. *Annals of the Association of American Geographers* 79, no. 1, 44–64.

Kane, Sally, John Reilly, and James Tobey. 1991. *Climate Change: Economic Implications for World Agriculture*. Resources and Technology Division, Economic Research Service, U.S. Department of Agriculture, Agricultural Economic Report no. 647 (October).

Kauppi, Pekka E., Kari Mielikäinen, and Kullervo Kuusela. 1992. Biomass and Carbon Budget of European Forests, 1971 to 1990. *Science* 256 (April 3): 70–74.

Keegan, John. 1993. *A History of Warfare*. New York: Alfred A. Knopf.

Kerr, Richard A. 1994. Climate Modeling's Fudge Factor Comes under Fire. *Science* 265 (September 9): 1528.

_____. 1995a. Study Unveils Climate Cooling Caused by Pollutant Haze. *Science* 268 (May 12): 802.

_____. 1995b. Studies Say—Tentatively—That Greenhouse Warming Is Here. *Science* 268 (June 16): 1567–68.

Kesseler, Adam T. 1994. Exciting Discoveries of Chinese Porcelain. Letter to the Editor, 1994. *Wall Street Journal* (May 31).

Knapp, P. A., and P. T. Soulé. 1996. Vegetation Change and the Role of Atmospheric CO_2 Enrichment on a Relict Site in Central Oregon: 1960–1994. *Annals of the Association of American Geographers* 86, no. 3, 387–411.

Ko-chen, Chu. 1973. A Preliminary Study on the Climatic Fluctuations during the Last 5,000 Years in China. *Scientia Sinica* 16, no. 2 (May).

Kremer, Michael. 1993. Population Growth and Technological Change: One Million B.C. to 1990. *Quarterly Journal of Economics* 108, no. 3 (August).

Ladurie, Emmanuel Le Roy. 1971. *Times of Feast, Times of Famine: A History of Climate since the Year 1000*. Garden City, N.Y.: Doubleday.

Lamb, Hubert H. 1968. *The Changing Climate*. London: Methuen.

_____. 1972. *Climate: Present, Past and Future, Fundamentals and Climate Now*. London: Methuen, vol. 1.

_____. 1977. *Climatic History and the Future*. Princeton, N.J.: Princeton University Press, vol. 2, 1985.

_____. 1982. *Climate, History and the Modern World*. New York: Methuen.

_____. 1988. *Weather, Climate & Human Affairs: A Book of Essays and Other Papers*. London and New York: Routledge.

Landsea, C. W. 1993. A Climatology of Intense (or Major) Atlantic Hurricanes. *Monthly Weather Review* 121, 1703–13.

Landsea, C. W., et al. 1996. Downward Trends in the Frequency of Intense Atlantic Hurricanes during the Past Five Decades. *Geophysical Research Letters* 23, 1697–1700.

Langer, William L. 1968. *An Encyclopedia of World History: Ancient, Medieval, and Modern Chronologically Arranged*. 4th ed. Boston: Houghton Mifflin.

Lancet. 1996. June 8, August 31.

Leary, N. 1994. The Amenity Value of Climate: A Review of Empirical Evidence from Migration, Wages, and Rents. Environmental Protection Agency, discussion paper.

Levenson, Thomas. 1989. *Ice Time: Climate, Science, and Life on Earth*. New York: Harper & Row.

Lindzen, Richard S. 1994. On the Scientific Basis for Global Warming Scenarios. *Environmental Pollution* 83, 125–34.

Lutter, Randall, and John Morrall. 1994. Health Analysis: A New Way to Evaluate Health and Safety Regulation 8, no. 1 (January): 43–66.

McGlone, Matt S., M. Jim Salinger, and Neville T. Moar. 1993. Paleovegetation Studies of New Zealand's Climate since the Last Glacial Maximum. In *Global Climates since the Last Glacial Maximum*. Edited by H. E. Wright Jr. et al. Minneapolis: University of Minnesota Press.

McKibbin, Warwick J., and Peter J. Wilcoxen. 1997. A Better Way to Slow Global Climate Change. Brookings Institution Policy Brief no. 17.

McNeill, William H. 1963. *The Rise of the West: A History of the Human Community.* Chicago: University of Chicago Press.

Mendelsohn, Robert, William D. Nordhaus, and Daigee Shaw. 1994. The Impact of Global Warming on Agriculture: A Ricardian Analysis. *American Economic Review* 84, no. 4 (September): 753–71

Michaels, Patrick. 1997. The Year in Review. *State of the Climate Report.* Charlottesville, Va.: New Hope Environmental Services, Inc.

Mitchell, George J. 1991. *World on Fire: Saving an Endangered Earth.* New York: Charles Scribner's Sons.

Moffat, Anne Simon. 1997. Resurgent Forests Can Be Greenhouse Gas Sponges. *Science* 277 (July 18): 315–16.

Momiyama, Masako. 1963. A Geographical Study of Seasonal Disease Calendar Model by Period and Country. *Papers in Meteorology and Geophysics* 14, 1–11.

———. 1977. *Seasonality in Human Mortality.* Tokyo: University of Tokyo.

Momiyama, Masako, and Kunie Katayama. 1967. A Medico-Climatological Study in the Seasonal Variation of Mortality in the United States of America (II). *Papers in Meteorology and Geophysics*, September, 209–32.

———. 1972. Deseasonalization of Mortality in the World. *International Journal of Biometeorology* 16, no. 4, 329–42.

Monastersky, R. 1994. Viking Teeth Recount Sad Greenland Tale. *Science News* 146 no. 20 (November 12): 310.

Moore, Thomas Gale. 1991. Central Planning USA-Style: The Case against Corporate Average Fuel Economy (CAFE) Standards. Hoover Essays Series in Public Policy.

———. 1995. Global Warming: A Boon to Humans and Other Animals. Hoover Essay Series.

———. 1998. Health and Amenity Effects of Global Warming. *Economic Inquiry.* Forthcoming.

Morley, Joseph J., and Beth A. Dworetzky. 1993. Holocene Temperature Patterns in the South Atlantic, Southern, and Pacific Oceans. In *Global Climates since the Last Glacial Maximum*. Edited by H. E. Wright Jr. et al. Minneapolis: University of Minnesota Press.

Myers, Norman. 1977. The Rich Diversity of Biodiversity Issues. In *Biodiversity II: Understanding and Protecting Our Biological Resources*. Edited by Marjorie L. Reaka-Kudla, Don E. Wilson, and Edward O. Wilson. Washington: Joseph Henry Press, 127.

Myneni, R. B., et al. 1997. Increased Plant Growth in the Northern High Latitudes from 1981 to 1991. *Nature* 386 (April 17).

National Center for Policy Analysis. 1996. *Brief Analysis* no. 213 (September 6).

References

National Oceanic and Atmospheric Administration (NOAA), National Climate Data Center. 1996. *Climate Variation Bulletin* (December).

_____. 1997. *Climate Variations Bulletin* 9, no. 2 (February).

National Research Council (NRC). 1978. *International Perspectives on the Study of Climate and Society*. Washington: National Academy Press.

_____, Committee on Science, Engineering, and Public Policy. 1991. *Policy Implications of Greenhouse Warming: Scientific Assessment*. Washington: National Academy Press.

Nerem, R. S. 1997. Global Mean Sea Level Change: Correction. *Science* 275, 1053.

Nicholls, N. 1992. Recent Performance of a Method for Forecasting Australian Seasonal Tropical Cyclone Activity. *Australian Meteorology Magazine* 40, 105–10.

Nicholls, Neville. 1997. Increased Australian Wheat Yield due to Recent Climate Trends. *Nature* 387 (May 29).

Nordhaus, William. 1991. To Slow or Not to Slow: The Economics of the Greenhouse Effect. *Economic Journal* 101 (July): 920–37.

_____. 1994. *Managing the Global Commons: The Economics of Climate Change*. Cambridge, Mass.: MIT Press.

Overpeck, Jonathan T. 1996. Warm Climate Surprises. *Science* 271 (March 29): 1820–21.

Pirenne, Henri. n.d., c. 1938. *Economic and Social History of Medieval Europe*. New York: Harcourt, Brace.

Rasool, S. I., and S. H. Schneider. 1971. Atmospheric Carbon Dioxide and Aerosols: Effects of Large Increases on Global Climate. *Science* 173 (July 9): 138–41.

Reaka-Kudla, Marjorie L., Don E. Wilson, and Edward O. Wilson, eds. 1977. *Biodiversity II: Understanding and Protecting Our Biological Resources*. Washington: Joseph Henry Press.

Rind, David. 1993. How Will Future Climate Changes Differ from Those of the Past? In *Global Changes in the Perspective of the Past*. Edited by J. A. Eddy and H. Oeschger. Somerset, N.J.: John Wiley and Sons.

Roback, Jennifer. 1988. Wages, Rents, and Amenities: Differences among Workers and Regions. *Economic Inquiry* 26, 23–41.

_____. 1982. Wages, Rents, and the Quality of Life. *Journal of Political Economy* 90 (December): 1257–79.

Rosen, Sherwin. 1979. Wages-based Indexes of Urban Quality of Life. In *Current Issues in Urban Economics*. Edited by Peter Mieszkowski and Mahlon Straszheim. Baltimore: Johns Hopkins University Press.

Rosenberg, Nathan and L. E. Birdzell Jr. 1986. *How the West Grew Rich: The Economic Transformation of the Industrial World*. New York: Basic Books.

Rosenthal, Donald H., Howard Gruenspecht, and Emily A. Moran. 1995. Effects of Global Warming on Energy Use for Space Heating and Cooling in the United States. *Energy Journal* 16, no. 2, 77–96.

Rotton, J. 1983. Angry, Sad, Happy? Blame the Weather. *U.S. News and World Report* 95, 52–53.

Schelling, Thomas C. 1992. Some Economics of Global Warming. *American Economic Review* 82 (March): 1–14.

Schneider, David. 1997. The Rising Seas. *Scientific American* (March): 112–17.

Shindell, Sidney, and Jack Raso. 1997. *Global Climate Change and Human Health*. New York: American Council on Science and Health.

Simpson, R. David, Roger A. Sedjo, and John W. Reid. 1996. Valuing Biodiversity for Use in Pharmaceutical Research. *Journal of Political Economy* 104, no. 1 (February): 163–85.

Smith, Adam. 1937. *The Wealth of Nations*. New York: Modern Library, Random House (1776).

Smith, Joel B., and Dennis Tirpak, eds. 1989. *The Potential Effects of Global Climate Change on the United States*. Environmental Protection Agency, Office of Policy, Planning and Evaluation, Office of Research and Development, Report to Congress.

Sohngen, Brent, and Robert Mendelsohn. 1996. Integrating Ecology and Economics: The Timber Market Impacts of Climate Change on U.S. Forests. Report Prepared for the Electric Power Research Institute Climate Change Impacts Program.

Stine, Scott. 1994. Extreme and Persistent Drought in California and Patagonia during Mediaeval Time. *Nature* 369 (June 16): 546–49.

Stone, Richard. 1995. Cities Could Face Killer Heat Waves. *Science* 267 (February 17): 958.

Sutherland, Ronald J. 1997. The Impact of Potential Climate Change Commitments on Energy Intensive Industries: A Delphi Analysis. Argonne National Laboratory, February 5.

Taubes, Gary. 1997. Apocalypse Not. *Science* (November 7): 1004–6.

Technological Review. 1989. November/December, 80.

Titus, J. G. 1992. The Cost of Climate Change to the United States. In *Global Climate Change: Implications, Challenges and Mitigation Measures*. Edited by S. K. Majumdar et al. Easton: Pennsylvania Academy of Science.

Tol, R. S. J. 1995. The Damage Costs of Climate Change: Towards More Comprehensive Calculations. *Environmental and Resource Economics* 5, 353–74.

Union of Concerned Scientists (UCS). 1997. The Present State of the Earth's Biodiversity. www.ucsusa.org/ucs.globalresources.html.

U.S. Department of Commerce. Various years. *Statistical Abstract of the United States*. Washington: Government Printing Office.

U.S. Department of State. 1997. U.S. Draft Protocol to the Framework Convention on Climate Change (January 28).

Van Doren, Charles. 1991. *A History of Knowledge: Past, Present, and Future*. New York: Ballantine Books.

Van Kooten, G. C. 1990. Climate Change Impacts on Forestry: Economic Issues. *Canadian Journal of Agricultural Economics* 38, 701–10.

Vigilant, Linda, et al. 1991. African Populations and the Evolution of Human Mitochondria DNA. *Science* (September 27): 1503–7.

Viscusi, W. Kip. 1994. Effects of Regulatory Costs and Policy Evaluation Criteria. *Rand Journal of Economics* 25, no. 1 (Spring): 94–109.

Webb, Thompson III, et al. 1993. Climatic Changes during the Past 18,000 Years: Regional Syntheses, Mechanisms, and Causes. In *Global Climates since the Last Glacial Maximum*. Edited by H. E. Wright Jr. et al. Minneapolis: University of Minnesota Press.

Weiner, J. S., et al. 1984. Heat-Associated Illnesses. In *Hunter's Tropical Medicine*, 6th ed. Edited by G. T. Strickland. Philadelphia: W. B. Saunders.

Wendland, Wayne M., and Reid A. Bryson. 1974. Dating Climatic Episodes of the Holocene. *Quaternary Research* 4, 9–24.

White, Margaret R., and I. Hertz-Picciotto. 1995. Human Health: Analysis of Climate Related to Health. In *Characterization of Information Requirements for Studies of CO_2 Effects: Water Resources, Agriculture, Fisheries, Forests and Human Health*. Edited by Margaret R. White. Washington: U.S. Department of Energy, Office of Energy Research.

Wigley, T. M. L., R. Richels, and J. A. Edmonds. 1996. Economic and Environmental Choices in the Stabilization of Atmospheric CO_2 Concentrations. *Nature* 379 (January 18): 240–43.

Wilson, Edward O. 1992. *The Diversity of Life*. Cambridge, Mass.: Harvard University Press.

Wittwer, S. H. 1995. *Food, Climate and Carbon Dioxide*. Boca Raton, Fla.: CRC Press.

_____. 1997. The Global Environment: It's Good for Food Production. In *State of the Climate Report*. Edited by P. J. Michaels. Arlington, Va.: New Hope Environmental Services, Western Fuels Association.

World Health Organization. 1990. *Potential Health Effects of Climate Change: Report of a WHO Task Group*. Geneva: World Health Organization.

_____. 1997. *World Health Report*. Geneva, Switzerland.

Yohe, Gary W. 1996. Climate Change Policies, the Distribution of Income, and U.S. Living Standards. Special Report, American Council for Capital Formation. Washington: Center for Policy Research (November).

Index

Aerosols
  in climate models, 10
  offset function of, 12, 19–20
  sulfate, 19
Agriculture
  feasibility and effect of, 31–32
  influence of climate change on, 113
  invention and use of, 39–40
  during Little Climate Optimum,
    50–51, 56–57
  medieval Europe (9th to 12th
    centuries), 49–50
  during Mini Ice Age, 62–67
  response to warmer weather, 104
  See also Animal domestication;
    Communities, fixed; Plant
    domestication
Air pollution
  effect of global warming on, 124
  presumed costs of increased, 109
  relation to mortality, 73
Allen, L. H., Jr., 114
Amenities
  amenity values theory, 90–91, 119
  effect of hot summers (Cline), 119
  environmental, 95–98
American Council on Science and
    Health, 70
Ammerman, Albert J., 30, 32, 40
Anderson, Christopher, 81, 121
Anderson, Robert J., Jr., 86–87
Animal domestication
  effect of, 33
  at end of last Ice Age, 31
  during Mini Ice Age, 63
  relation to agriculture and climate
    change, 40–42, 67
Animals
  response to climate change, 95–98
  value of, 98–102
Antarctic, the
  effect of ice buildup, 21
  during First Climatic Optimum, 39
  glaciers of, 14
Applegate, W. B., 73

Aquinas, Thomas, 56
Arctic, the
  during Little Climate Optimum,
    56–57
  ocean and ice, 14
Arrhenius, Svante, 9
Arriaga-Salinas, A. S., 90, 93
Atmosphere
  components of, 10
  cooling after Mt. Pinatubo eruption,
    13, 19
Ausubel, Jesse H., 15, 17

Bacon, Roger, 56
Baker, J. T., 114
Bartlett, Robert, 47, 49, 50, 51, 54
Beckerman, Wilfred, 156
Bell, Frederick W., 126
Benkovic, S. R., 21
Bentley, Charles R., 14
Berlin Mandate (1995), 6, 131
Bernstein, Paul M., 144
Biodiversity
  contributions of, 98
  measuring value of, 99
Biodiversity Convention, 100
Birdzell, L. E. , Jr., 66
Blair, Tony, 136, 138
Blomquist, Glenn C., 90, 91, 93
Bolin, Bert, 1, 143, 150
Boserup, Ester, 31, 32, 35
Bridger, C. A., 73
Broccoli, Anthony J., 25
Broderick, Anthony, 105
Browne, Malcolme W., 17
Browner, Carol M., 5
Bryson, Reid A., 31
Bull, G. M., 82, 83
Bush administration, 5

California Floristic province, 102
Carbon dioxide (CO_2)
  benefits from increased, 113–17, 128
  as component of earth's atmosphere,
    10–11

concentrations in atmosphere, 14–15
effect on forestry of increased, 116–17
environment with higher levels of, 97
estimates of effect of doubled (Nordhaus), 108–9
heating effect of, 10–13
historical levels of, 27–37
levels during Climatic Optimum, 37–43
restrictions negotiated at Kyoto (1997), 132, 134
Carbon dioxide (CO$_2$) emissions
costs to curb, 154
effect of, 10–12
forecasts of, 14–16
proposed tax to curb, 135–36
Carpenter, Ray, 44
Carruth, Gorton, 56, 58, 60, 67
Cavalli-Sforza, L. L., 30, 32, 40
Chao, Kang, 48, 57–58, 66
Chapman, Kenneth S., 154
Cheetham, Nicolas, 45, 52, 66
Chirac, Jacques, 136, 138
Chlorofluorocarbons (CFCs)
effect of, 10–13
phasing out of, 3, 11–12, 155
Circumpolar vortex
expansion after High Middle Ages, 62
function and effect of, 21
probable effect of global warming on, 82
Civilizations
Americas during Litle Climate Optimum, 59–60
Harappans, 43
Claiborne, Robert, 38, 39, 43, 45, 51
Climate
effect of clouds on, 19
during Little Climate Optimum, 46–60
post-Climatic Optimum, 43–46
predicted effect of greenhouse gases on, 13–14
predictions of regional, 19
preferences for, 85–86, 89
role in human activity, 27
variability, 14
See also Climatic Optimum; Little Climate Optimum
Climate, cooler
effect (A.D. 550–1000), 45–46
at end of Climatic Optimum, 43–46

See also Global cooling; Ice Age; Mini Ice Age
Climate, warmer
benefits of moderately, 87–88, 118–28
effect (A.D. 1000–1300), 45–60
effect on mortality rates, 120
effect on weather, 21–23
evidence of periods of, 35–43
gains from, 4
See also Global warming
Climate change
assumptions of gradual, 14
economic forecasts of influence of, 3–4
effect of, 26
estimates of damage from, 153
estimates of influence on agriculture, 113–16
estimates of influence on forestry, 113, 116–17
estimates of influence on transportation, 113, 124–26
evidence of, 23–26
health effects of, 72
historical evidence of, 23–37
implications for U.S. economy and people's well-being, 86
IPCC prediction of gradual, 96
during Mini Ice Age, 60–67
predictions of insect-borne diseases with, 75–78
prophets of, 1–2
related to invention of agriculture, 39
Climate Change Action Plan, 5
Climate models
predictions of, 17–18, 21
replication capabilities, 17
uncertainty of, 9–10, 18–21
Climatic Optimum
expansion of civilization during, 42–43
source of, 28
temperatures during, 25
weather, precipitation, and temperatures during, 37–43
See also Little Climate Optimum
Cline, William, 69, 70, 104, 109–12, 117–19, 123–24, 126–27
Clinton, William J.
criticism of, 136
on global warming, 1
position on reduction of carbon emissions, 133–34

Clinton administration
  Climate Change Action Plan, 5
  plan to cut CO₂ emissions, 132
  position on aims of FCCC, 5
  position on Kyoto agreement, 143–44
Cogen, Douglas, 9
Cohen, Mark, 32, 36–37
Colwell, Rita R., 78–80
Communities, fixed, 41
Conference of Parties (COP), 5
Cook, Edward, 59
COP. *See* Conference of Parties (COP).
Cost/benefit analysis, 6–7
Crandall, Robert W., 131
Cropper, M. L., 90, 93
Cross, Frank B., 154
Crowley, Thomas J., 24, 27, 28, 29

Danzig, David, 75
D'Arge, Ralph, 86, 92, 106t
Davis, Robert E., 21, 73, 74, 83
Deland, Antoinette, 59
Dingell, John, 139
Disease
  causes of chronic, 69
  cholera, 78–81
  during Mini Ice Age, 63–66
  predictions of insect-borne, 75–78
Donkin, R. A., 50, 54, 63
Downer, Alexander, 139
Drake, Judith, 90, 92
Duleep, Harriet O., 154
Dworetzky, Beth A., 29

Eaton, Robert, 129
Economic activity
  climate effects on, 103
  Europe during Little Climate
    Optimum, 48–56
  Far East during Little Climate
    Optimum, 57–59
  growth of five industrialized
    countries (1992–97), 137–39
  with mechanisms to control
    emissions, 143–50
  during Mini Ice Age, 60–67
Ehrlich, Paul, 100
Ellis, F. P., 73, 83
El Niño, 80–81
Energy
  energy-saving policies, 130–31
  estimates of savings with global
    warming, 118–19
  uses under Kyoto agreement, 146–50

Epstein, Paul, 75
European Union (EU)
  proposal to reduce CO₂ emissions,
    135, 136
  reduced greenhouse gases in, 137–38

Fairbridge, R. W., 62
Famine, 64–67
Fisher, Brian, 144
Flohn, H., 25
Folland, C. K., 82
Forestry
  influence of climate change on, 113,
    116–18
Framework Convention on Climate
    Change (FCCC)
  Conference of Parties (COP), 5–6
  secretariat, 5
Frankhauser, S., 127t
Free rider problems, 7
Frenzel, Burkhard, 25, 28

Gates, W. L., 82
Giles, Bill, 27, 38, 82
Gimpel, Jean, 53, 65
Glaciers
  Antarctica, 14
  Greenland, 14
  during last Ice Age, 30
  during Mini Ice Age, 62
Global commons, 7
Global cooling
  after High Middle Ages, 61–67
  speculation related to, 17
  worries about (1970s), 2
Global warming
  benefits from, 112t, 126–27
  conditions leading to predictions of,
    73–74
  estimates of cost of (Cline; Moore),
    111–12, 127–28
  estimates of effects (Cline), 109–13
  evidence related to hypothesis of,
    9–10
  forecasts of future, 18
  IPCC forecasts (1990s), 13
  politics of, 136–43
  predicted health effects of, 75–78
  predictions of, 13–14
  predictions of EPA climate change
    study, 107
  uncertainty related to, 14–16
Global warming models, 21

Gore, Al, 60, 69, 152
  actions and speech at Kyoto, 141
  on effects of climate change, 4, 24
  on effects of higher world
    temperatures, 38
  imagined threat of global warming,
    1, 4
Graham, John D., 131
Graves, Philip E., 90
Greenhouse gas emissions
  cooperation to curb, 153
  cost to prevent buildup of, 150–54
  forecasts of Kyoto agreement, 143–46
  international pressures to reduce, 5
  proposals to reduce, 132–34
Greenhouse gases
  Berlin Mandate related to reduction
    of, 131
  climatic effect, 11–13
  debate over effect of, 3
  increase in levels of, 10–12, 14–15
  sources, effect, and absorption of,
    10–13
  Wirth proposal to reduce, 132
  See also Carbon dioxide (CO$_2$);
    Chlorofluorocarbons (CFCs);
    Methane (CH$_4$)
Group of 77, 141
Gyourko, Joseph, 90, 92, 93

Hallam, H. E., 49
Hard, Thomas M., 105
Hariharan, Govind, 154
Healy, Melissa, 1
Hertz-Picciotto, I., 71, 113
Hoch, Irving, 90, 92
Horwitz, Lawrence M., 132, 146
Howard, John, 138–39
Huggett, Richard John, 24
Humans
  with advent of agriculture, 32–43
  during Climatic Optimum period, 31
  effect of climate warming on, 89–90
  effects of climate on health, 69–88
  health with warmer climate, 120–21
  influence of climate on well-being of,
    26–37
  during last Ice Age, 29–32
  response to climate, 27

Ice Age, last
  agriculture invented at end of, 39
  climate changes during, 25
  conditions during, 30–31

  weather, precipitation, and
    temperatures during, 39
  See also Mini Ice Age
Industrialized countries
  under Kyoto agreement, 143–50
  mandate to reduce emissions, 5,
    141–42
  response to warmer climate, 103–4
Innes, J. L., 116–17
Intergovernmental Panel on Climate
    Change (IPCC)
  assumptions related to emissions
    forecasts, 16–17, 129
  predictions related to temperature
    increases, 3, 9–10, 13, 87
  summary of atmospheric
    concentrations (1992), 20t
  Working Group I forecasts, 13, 20
  Working Group II, 69
  Working Group III, 112–13, 153

Jet stream. See Circumpolar vortex.
Johnson, Kenneth S., 156
Justus, John, 10, 11

Kalkstein, Laurence, 70, 72, 73, 74, 83
Kane, Sally, 113, 115
Katayama, Kunie, 82
Kauppi, Pekka E., 11
Keegan, John, 46, 48, 55
Kerr, Richard A., 10, 12, 18
Kesseler, Adam, 58
Knapp, Paul, 114
Ko-chen, Chu, 43, 48
Kohl, Helmut, 136
Kremer, Michael, 33–34, 66
Kyoto protocol (1997), 6–8, 131–32, 134

Ladurie, Emmanuel LeRoy, 67
Lamb, Hubert H., 10, 31, 35f, 37–39,
    41–48, 51, 55, 56–57, 59, 60–66, 82
Landsea, C. W., 21–22
Land values, 91–92, 115, 118
Langer, William L., 55, 58, 60, 63
Leary, N., 119
Less-developed countries
  economic activity under Kyoto
    agreement, 147
  exemption from reduction of
    emissions, 5–6, 134–35, 143–46
Levenson, Thomas, 24
Life expectancy
  evidence for different periods, 34–36
  during warmest periods, 35

Lindzen, Richard, 3, 9, 18
Little Climate Optimum
   economic activity during, 48–59
   mild winters during, 25, 46–60
   population growth in Europe, 48–51
   temperature and climate during,
      46–60
Lovejoy, Thomas E., 98
Lutter, Randall, 120

McGlone, Matt S., 29, 43
McKibbin, Warwick J., 152
McNeill, William H., 56, 58
Mencken, H. L., 1
Mendelsohn, Robert, 113, 115, 116
Methane (CH₄)
   as component of earth's atmosphere,
      10–13
   contribution of emissions to earth's
      warming, 10–11
Michaels, Patrick, 3, 10
Mini Ice Age
   agriculture during, 62–67
   availability of food during, 36–37
   economic activity, climate change,
      and weather during, 60–67
   effect in the Arctic, 56–57
   famine during, 64–67
   start and spread of, 48
   temperature during, 31, 34, 60–67
Mitchell, George J., 23, 69
Moffat, Anne Simon, 157
Momiyama, Masako, 82, 83
Monastersky, R., 63
Montreal Protocol, 3, 155
Moore, Thomas Gale, 34f, 83–85, 93,
   127t, 131
Morley, Joseph J., 29
Morrall, John, 120
Morrissey, Wayne, 10, 11
Mortality
   effects of temperature change on
      incidence of, 72–75
   factors affecting, 85
   incidence during winter and
      summer, 83
   with warmer climate, 120
Morton, Joan, 82, 83
Myers, Norman, 96–97
Myneni, R. B., 11, 96, 104, 114

National Research Council (NRC), 2,
   10, 69, 109

criticism of IPCC predictions, 9–10
   estimates of CO₂ emissions, 12
Nerem, R. S., 21
Nicholls, Neville, 22, 96, 114
Nordhaus, William, 70, 108–9, 113, 115,
   127t, 146
No-regrets policy, 2, 130–31
North, Gerald, 24, 29

Organisation for Economic Cooperation
   and Development (OECD)
   proposal to reduce CO₂ emissions,
      135
Overpeck, Jonathan T., 13
Ozone layer, 11

Patrick, Ruth, 98
Pirenne, Henri, 49, 51, 54, 65
Plant domestication
   effect of, 33
   at end of last Ice Age, 31
   related to warmer climate, 39–40, 67
Plants
   response to climate change, 95–98
   response to higher CO₂ levels, 104,
      113–17
   value of, 98–102
Population decline
   during Mini Ice Age, 63–67
Population growth
   with advent of agriculture, 41
   with climate warming, 32–34, 61
   in Europe during Little Climate
      Optimum, 48–51
   post-11th century, 48–49
Precautionary principle, 154–56
Precipitation
   during Climatic Optimum, 37–43, 67
   Cline's estimates based on global
      warming, 110
   Cline's forecasts, 109–13
   rainfall during Little Climate
      Optimum, 46–48
Preferences
   amenity value theory, 90–91, 119
   climate-related, 85–86, 89, 119–20
   wage-related, 92–95
Property rights concept, 41–42
Public policy
   cost/benefit analysis to evaluate, 6–7
   fashioning, 156–58
   issues related to emission reduction,
      6–8
   of "no-regrets," 2, 130–31

regulatory constrainsts of, 130–31
with significant warming, 3

Quotas, marketable
emission reduction certificates, 152
to meet emission limits of Kyoto
protocol, 8, 134, 152

Rainfall. *See* Precipitation.
Raso, Jack, 70
Rasool, S. I., 2
Reaka-Kudla, Marjorie L., 98
Reid, John, 101–2
Resources for the Future, 101–2
Rind, David, 24, 25, 28
Rio conference (1992)
Biodiversity Convention, 100
Framework Convention on Climate
Change, 5
position of industrialized countries
at, 7
Roback, Jennifer, 90, 91, 92–93
Rosen, Sherwin, 90
Rosenberg, Nathan, 66
Rosenthal, Donald H., 119
Rotton, J., 73

Santer, Benjamin, 1
Schelling, Thomas, 127
Schneider, David, 20
Schneider, S. H., 1,2
Sea levels
after High Middle Ages, 62
with end of last Ice Age, 31
estimates of effect of global warming
on, 14, 118
factors influencing, 14–15
during First Climatic Optimum,
37–39
forecasts and costs of rising, 13–14,
104
with global warming, 153
during Little Climate Optimum, 51
during Mini Ice Age, 62
during periods of cooler
temperatures, 44
during periods of warmer
temperatures, 43, 51–52
predicted rise in, 23
uncertainty about future, 14–16
Sedjo, Roger, 101–2
Shaw, Daigee, 113, 115
Shindell, Sidney, 70
Simpson, R. David, 101–2

Singer, S. Fred, 3
Smith, Adam, 90
Smith, Joel B., 70, 107
Sohngren, Brent, 116
Soulé, Peter, 114
Specialization
in fixed communities, 41
Species
effect of climate change on, 95–98
estimates of effect of global warming
on, 117–18
See also Animals; Biodiversity; Plants
Stine, Scott, 47
Stone, Richard, 70
Sutherland, Ronald J., 148

Taubes, Gary, 70
Taxation
in Clinton proposal to reduce CO_2
emissions, 132–33, 151–52
in EU proposal to reduce CO_2
production, 135, 136
to meet Kyoto protocol emission
limits, 7
in OECD proposal to reduce CO_2
emissions, 135
Technology
during High Middle Ages, 54–56
innovations during Climatic
Optimum, 42
during Little Climate Optimum,
46–60
during Mini Ice Age, 65
with population growth, 33–34
at times of climate change, 26
Temperature
during Climatic Optimum, 37–43
effect on forestry of increased,
116–17
effect on humans, 29
effect on levels of air pollution, 124
forecasted effects of rising, 69
IPCC estimates of increased, 153
during Little Climate Optimum,
46–60
measurement of, 17–21
during Mini Ice Age, 31, 34, 60–67
post-Climatic Optimum variation, 43
related to mortality, 72–75, 82–87
Tirpak, Dennis, 70, 107
Titus, J. G., 127t
Tol, R. S. J., 127t
Tracy, Joseph, 90, 92, 93

Trade
during Climatic Optimum, 42, 67
during Little Climate Optimum, 49
Transportation
influence of climate change on, 113–16

Union of Concerned Scientists (UCS), 99–100
United Nations Framework Convention on Climate Change (FCCC) (1992), 5
U.S. Department of Energy
estimates of compliance with CO_2 reduction schemes, 148–50
estimates of energy savings, 119
U.S. Department of Transportation
research related to climate, 2, 85–86
study on implications of climate change (1974), 104–5, 106t
U.S. Environmental Protection Agency (EPA)
global climate change study, 105–7
greenhouse gas emissions study, 105–6
projected cost of rise in sea levels, 107–8

Van Doren, Charles, 52
Van Kooten, G. C., 116

Vigilant, Linda, 29
Viscusi, W. Kip, 120

Waldman, Donald M., 90
Water pollution, 110
Watson, Robert, 1
Weather
effects on incidence of mortality, 72–73
during Mini Ice Age, 61–67
pleasant, 89
predicted effects of climate change on, 21–23
with warmer climate, 121–22
Webb, Thompson III, 28–29
Well-being, human, 26–37
Wendland, Wayne M., 31
White, Margaret R., 71, 113
Wigley, T. M., 151
Wilcoxen, Peter J., 152
Willingness-to-pay concept, 99, 117
Wilson, Edward O., 95
Wirth, Timothy, 6, 132
Wittwer, S. H., 104, 113–14, 115–16

Yohe, Gary W., 132, 147, 154

About the Author

Thomas Gale Moore is a senior fellow at the Hoover Institution at Stanford University and was a member of the President's Council of Economic Advisers between 1985 and 1989. He is the author of numerous books and scholarly articles on transportation, economics, and climate change. Before coming to Hoover, Dr. Moore was a professor of economics at Michigan State University where he taught economic theory and industrial organization. He has also taught at the Carnegie Institute of Technology, the Stanford University Graduate School of Business, and UCLA. He lives in Palo Alto, California.